Growing Up on a Nebraska Farm

H. LYNN BECK

Growing Up on a Nebraska Farm

Copyright © 2022 by H. Lynn Beck.

PB: ISBN: 978-1-63812-378-1
Ebook ISBN: 9978-1-63812-379-8

All rights reserved. No part in this book may be produced and transmitted in any form or by any means, electronic, or mechanical, including photocopying, recording, or by any information storage and retrieval system, without permission in writing from the copyright owner.

*The views expressed in this work are solely those of the author and do not necessarily reflect the views of the publisher hereby disclaims any responsibility for them.
Published by Pen Culture Solutions 07/18/2022*

*Pen Culture Solutions
1-888-727-7204 (USA)
1-800-950-458 (Australia)
support@penculturesolutions.com*

Contents

1949 (January)—Eighteen Months Old. 1
    A Cold Winter. 1
    The Barn Dance 2
    1950—Three Years Old. 3
    First Memories. 3
    The Farm. 4
    Farm Chores. 4
    Irrigation. 5
    Grandpa Tyler's Irrigation Innovation. 7
1951—Four Years Old. 8
1952—Five Years Old. 9
    The Farm. 9
    My First Plowing Experience. 10
    Chores. 11
    Land Leveling. 12
    One Room Country School House. .12
    The Squirrel. 16
    Corn Incident with Shannon. 17
    Bootsy. 18
    The Castor Oil Caper. 19
    Grandma's and Grandpa's Place. 19
    Our Christmas Celebration. 22
1953 (6 years old). 24
    Sheri Was Born. 24
    Putting Up Hay. 24
    Shannon and the Elevator Spring Caper. 26
    Doc Douglas. 27
    Doc Shaw. 28

The Wagon Incident with Shannon.	28
Saturday Night.	28
The Sow Stampede.	29
1954 (7 years old).	**33**
Land Leveling.	33
Threshing Oats.	35
First Television Set.	36
Shannon Falls from Wagon Wheel.	36
1955 (eight years old, third grade).	**37**
Going To Lubbock, Texas for Scraper Parts.	37
1956 (nine years old, fourth grade).	**38**
Land Leveling.	38
Irrigation.	40
Chores.	41
Corn Shelling.	42
Church.	43
Underground Fort.	44
The New Machine Shed.	45
1957 (ten years old, fifth grade).	**46**
Bootsy Died.	46
Dad Bought a New Quarter (his second).	46
A Wet Spring.	47
Tilling the Set Aside Acres.	48
Land Leveling.	48
Irrigation.	50
My New Friends, Gordon and Tippy.	52
New School in Town.	54
End of Irrigating Season.	55
Putting Up Silage.	55
Mom Slaughters Broiler Hens.	56
Dad Builds a Swimming Pool.	57

- Hunting Pheasants and Quail with Grandpa Tyler..............58
- Hunting Ducks and Geese with Grandpa Tyler...............58
- End-of-Year Special Employee Dinner......................61
- Playing in the Haymow...................................61
- Packing Grease in Ball Bearings..........................62

1958 (11 years old, 6th grade)..........................62
- Dad Bought Another Quarter (3rd Quarter)................62
- The Spring Harrow.......................................63
- First Color Television Set..............................63
- Sherilyn Swims in Deep End of Pool......................64
- Wheat Harvest...64
- Uncle Wayne Cuts Our Hair...............................65
- Land Leveling...65
- George Fell from Pickup.................................66
- Late Corn Hilling.......................................67
- Harvesting and Selling Watermelons......................68
- Digging Grandpa's Potatoes..............................68
- Replacing Bicycle Flat Tires............................69
- The Lost Milk Cows......................................70
- Cutting Wood for Furnace................................74
- Grandpa and His Wood Working............................76

1959 (12 years old, 7th grade)..........................77
- More Land Added (4th Quarter)...........................77
- Cutting Stalks..78
- Cultivating with Gordon.................................79
- Richard Timmons, Chemist................................79
- Taking a Lawn Mower Apart...............................81
- The Milk and Cream Experiment...........................82
- Enter Hayes Randall.....................................82
- My Legs Were Caught in Ford Tractor's Tires.............83

Uncle Wayne's Lake and Sunday Fun 84
　　Grandpa Tyler and Fireworks 85
　　Grandpa Tyler's Orchard 86
　　Dad Burns Weeds 86
　　Dad Built Grain Bins and Storage Units 87
　　Converting from Corn Picker to Combine 87
　　Helping Clark Williams Harvest Corn 88
　　Grade School Basketball 89
　　Dick Vincent Joins the Scraper Team 90
　　Emptying the Grain Quonset 90
　　I Was Nearly Electrocuted 91
　　Visitors from the City 91
1961 (14 years old, Freshman) 93
　　Loading the Corn Planter 93
　　Shop Teacher Worked for Dad 93
　　I Entered High School 94
　　Leslie Receives Driver's License 94
　　Land Leveling 95
　　The Spanish Book 95
　　Fixing the Brake on a JD B 96
1963 (16 years old, Sophomore) 97
　　A Summer's Date 97
　　Dad Sells the Milk Cows 97
　　Leslie Graduates from High School 98
1964 (16 years old, Junior in High School) 98
　　We Buy More Land (5th and 6th Quarters) 98
　　High School Bomb Making 99
1965 (17 years old, Senior) 100
　　Unloading Trucks during School Time 100

Irrigation 100
Post High School Graduation. 100
George Takes Care of My Sisters. 101

Dedication

I want to thank my siblings: Leslie, Shannon, Shelli, and Sheri, for helping recall stories from our deep past. I also want to thank my cousins: Kathy, Dan, and Brian for adding to these stories about Grandpa and Grandma Tyler.

1949 (January) — Eighteen Months Old

A Cold Winter

Every fall, Dad went to a cattle auction in Broken Bow to buy weaned calves from the western ranches that had cow-calf operations. Dad did this so the weaned calves could pick up ears of corn dropped in the field by the picker, or that nature had knocked down. It also allowed him to maintain George, our hired man, the entire year. It was George's job during the late fall and twinter to grind corn, mix it with other nutritional ingredients, and feed it to the steers. Also, he had to keep on the lookout for sick animals and keep the water tanks as free from ice as possible. The winter that year had been very cold and snowy. George had been miserable feeding the steers every day with the north winds blowing down.

On January 2nd, a northern storm approached. At that time there was no reliable storm warning systems, and we did not yet own a television. Dad went to bed apprehensive. It started to snow heavily in the early evening and did not stop until January 6th. As we slept, the snow accumulated, and the wind howled menacingly. In the morning, George came dressed for the cold. He had multiple layers of clothing that weighed heavily on his shoulders. It was still snowing mightily, and the wind was still howling. When George went to feed the cattle, he noticed they were mostly gone. Only a few steers remained in the corral. When he investigated, he found that snowdrifts made from very wet, heavy snow covered the fences, and the cattle simply walked out of the corral. It was the same for the neighbors.

Dad and George each grabbed a tractor and started driving around the farm looking for the missing animals. They started finding our animals and animals from other farms. They drove them back to the corral and separated our animals from the neighbors' animals. George grabbed small steel posts and secured them to the wooden corral posts. He then strung electric fence wire and electrified the fence on top of the wooden fence. It worked. No more cattle escaped.

Before George could feed the animals, he had to unhook the grinder from the John Deere 60 (JD60), which had a loader attached. He proceeded to clean the snow in front of the feeder troughs so that the tractor and grinder could pass by, unload grain into the trough, and behind it so that the cattle could walk up to the trough, and be able to stick their heads through a slot to eat. This done, he again hooked up the grinder and fed the animals while Dad continued to drive around looking for animals. Dad found more animals and met neighbors who had some of Dad's animals. Eventually, they found the missing animals and exchanged them until everyone was happy.

The Barn Dance

Since the heavy snow paralyzed the region, Dad's cousin, who lived a mile away, decided to have a barn dance. He called all neighbors within a reasonable radius and invited them to his barn in the heavy snow. He cleaned the haymow by pushing back the residual loose straw that had accumulated from the years of straw bales being tossed about. He swept the floor as clean as was possible and placed fresh straw bales around for people to sit on. He placed strings of lights around what was to be the dance floor.

Mom prepared sandwiches and a thermos of coffee. Dad found an old toboggan and placed layers of cardboard on the bottom before situating the food, coffee, and me, and we were off. Leslie, who was four years old, walked as far as he could. Then he joined me on the toboggan, which Dad pulled. The trip did not take as long as one might think. Time passed quickly as Leslie was jumping and playing as he went.

Arriving at the barn, we went up the stairs to the haymow and found women talking excitedly while laying out the food and drinks. The men mostly talked about their cattle escaping from their corrals and the seriousness of the blizzard. The children who could walk and run were walking and running around. Leslie climbed onto straw bales and jumped off, then he found bales stacked two high and jumped again. A haymow was a gigantic playground. Mom wrapped me warmly and placed in an area Mom and Dad had claimed when they arrived.

Then the dancing started. The couples gathered and they danced for hours. Once they paused to eat and drink coffee and then they continued dancing. Little by little, we smaller children tired and made nests near the area claimed by our moms and dads, and we slept.

Once or twice, I awoke and found myself on the cardboard covered toboggan. Then I was home and in bed. I was exhausted.

Later in the year, the family grew when Shannon was born on October 8th, 1949.

1950—Three Years Old

First Memories

My next memories were from a fall day. My five-year-old brother was at kindergarten, and I was bored. I had no one to play with. I went outside and was attracted by what George was doing. He was unloading recently picked corn into a large wooden corncrib. A John Deere B tractor was using its power-take-off (PTO) to turn the chain on the ear corn elevator. The elevator itself was long and placed at a steep angle to reach the opening in the top of the roof. Sometimes, when an ear was being elevated, gravity would work on it and pull it back. Usually, the ear found traction and continued its trek to the top of the corn crib. However, some ears fell to the ground.

I walked to the wagon being unloaded and looked for George. He was no where to be found. The PTO transferring the JD B's power to the large bicycle-like chain, which turned the wheel that turned the paddles carrying the corn ears upwards, was spinning very rapidly. The PTO was a straight shaft. It had no safety features that all PTO's have today. If it caught your arm, you would lose your arm. If it caught your clothing, and you were lucky, it would strip your clothes from your body before you knew what was happening. If you were not lucky, the accident would be fatal.

It was in this environment that I saw an ear of corn that had fallen from the corn elevator and lay on the ground underneath the elevator. I wanted to help, so I reached in and recovered the ear. The shortest distance to the ear was achieved by reaching between the chains. As I slowly removed the ear from between the two sides of the large bicycle chain, I misjudged, and my hand was caught in the chain. It pulled my hand between the chain and the sprocket. It caught, and severed, the tips of two fingers. My fingers started bleeding profusely.

I walked the hundred feet to the house, holding my wounded hand up because it hurt less when I did. Our house had the main floor elevated six feet from ground level. The kitchen was directly in the front of the house so that Mom could look out the window and have an idea of what was going on. I stopped at the door and looked up at the kitchen window, crying loudly while holding my arm, which by this time, was all red. After what seemed like an eternity, she appeared. I remember she was drying her hands on a towel. She looked first towards the machinery and saw nothing. Then, she looked down and her mouth fell open in astonishment. I remember no more. I was three years old.

The Farm

Dad owned 160 acres and rented another 160 acres from Grandpa Beck. He produced mostly corn with wheat and alfalfa. Dad dedicated twenty acres to pasture for the milk cows. He usually maintained ten to fifteen cows. Ten were usually fresh and needed to be milked twice a day. He had two John Deere B's (JD Bs), one for George and one for himself. These tractors could pull a two-row planter, go-dig, and cultivator. The JD Bs only had twelve horsepower, but they had good traction. Dad was ambitious and intended on increasing the size of his farm either by adding more land or by making the existing land more productive.

Farm Chores

I was three years old and had no chores, but Mom and Dad gave Leslie responsibility for caring for the chickens. This consisted of watering them, feeding them and collecting eggs, which had to be taken to our basement where they were cleaned and placed into a large thirty-six dozen box. Later, the cooperative would pass buy and collect the eggs once a week.

Irrigation

Many, but not all, farms had some irrigation. Irrigation wells were placed here and there either based on convenience (like on a field's corner for easy access) and hope that water would be found, or by a process called water witching. Water witching could place pumps in the middle of a field, or in some odd place in the field, all according to the results of how two wires behaved in the hands of the water witcher. He loosely held two wires bent in the shape of an L and walked around holding the wires out in his hands. When they both moved, hopefully a water vein had been located and they sunk a well.

One pump could irrigate about forty acres. Since the farms were in the Platte River valley, the water level was never very deep, usually between ten and twenty feet. The soil was not good at retaining water because it was sandy. We had to irrigate corn about every five days. Each year, we irrigated the crops between fifteen and twenty times.

To carry the water from the pump into the fields, Dad made ditches in the sandy soil and ran them around the field while he attempted to follow a contour with a small downward gradient to help the water flow down the ditch. Every hundred feet, or so, we constructed a dirt dam using a spade. When the water filled the ditch, we made even cuts in about ten rows. We made the cuts in every other row because the water running down the row watered the corn on both sides. We made these cuts with a spade. They always attempted to make the flow from the ditch in every row even so the water would arrive at each row's end at the same time. However, after an hour or two, some rows were blocked by dirt falling from the ditch's side into the cut and blocking the water. The water level would rise a little, increasing the flow in the remaining rows. Sometimes the water concentrated its flow in one row. This was known as a ditch-break.

This type of irrigation was problematic and labor intensive. Dad had to check each set of rows often to avoid wasting water and to keep the rows flowing as evenly as possible. When one row flowed as far as gravity could take it, we had close it, allowing more water to flow into the remaining rows. Once all rows were "down," or the water from all rows had gone as far as they could, we closed that set, and we opened a new set of rows. Eventually, we replaced the dirt dam with another one, a hundred feet down the ditch.

Dad had to discover how far the water had flowed and mark down the status of each row. This was complicated, time consuming, and required much walking.

The irrigated part of the field had tall stalks of corn. Where the water did not reach, the corn had leaves that were brown in the center with the bottom several leaves burned and dropping to the ground. Their ears of corn were small and poorly pollinated. This was what happened to dryland corn in the Platte River valley.

To keep the pumps working, Dad often made sets during the night. He wore a miner-type flashlight with the bulb secured around his forehead. This freed his hands for the spade. Sometimes he would sleep in a row as far down as the water could flow, leaving his arm in the bottom of the row where the water would be running. When the water reached as far as it could go, it covered his hand and woke him. He walked back to the ditch and changed the irrigation set.

Leslie often accompanied Dad and helped as much as a five-year-old could help. Sometimes he held an extra flashlight or helped in any way that Dad asked.

Dad wanted to irrigate each stalk of corn that could be reached. Sometimes a small hump existed in the field that stopped the flow of water. If the hump were not there, the water could flow farther and reach more corn. He took a spade and dug the bottoms of the rows as much as six inches deeper to help the water flow farther down the row. He napped in the pickup between times. He spent more time in the pickup than he did in bed.

Grandpa Tyler's Irrigation Innovation

Grandpa Tyler's farm bordered the Platte River, consequently the soil was very sandy. This made growing a corn crop exceedingly difficult. In 1938, he reasoned that he should be able to capture water from near the river to irrigate, even though his land was uneven. This became his goal.

He found an old sandpit pump for sale for one-hundred dollars, but he did not have the money. He went to his banker for the money. The banker denied the loan. He told Grandpa that he would loan Grandpa money to buy cattle or machinery, but not for irrigation. He continued to lecture Grandpa that irrigation had no future in the region.

Grandpa returned home and started saving money. He saved money from chicken eggs, but mostly from selling watermelons. Grandpa loved watermelons and had had a watermelon patch since he was a kid. He saved seed from the good melons and replanted them the following year. Grandpa became well known for his watermelons. People came from several towns over to buy them. They came mostly Saturdays and Sundays when town people did not have to work. Grandpa had collected a couple of horse wagons filled with melons from the field the day before. He had them parked under a giant tree, which had an old balance hung from a low and sturdy branch. Grandpa could weigh three or four melons at a time. His business was always brisk. From these sales, he saved as much money as he could. Finally, one day, he had the one-hundred dollars, and he bought the pump.

Grandpa attached an old horse-drawn scraper to a small tractor. His son, Wayne, drove the tractor while Grandpa stood behind the scraper and held the wooden handles. By pushing down or up on the handles, Grandpa determined how deep the scraper would dig and when it would stop digging. They dragged the sand a few yards and deposited it, forming a small pile. After digging below the water level, which was only a couple of feet, Grandpa placed the pump into the hole. He turned the tractor around and hooked the tractor's pulley to the pump's pulley. After a brief second of pumping air, water gushed from the pump. Grandpa was happy.

At that time Uncle Wayne was a young man. After he graduated from high school, he attended winter agricultural extension classes at the University of Nebraska. One of the classes he took showed him how to survey by using a level and a transit. He found a level and with it, located the highest point in the field. Grandpa laid a pipe to transport the water to that point.

To place the water distributing ditch, Uncle Wayne mapped a contour from the highest point with a gently decreasing gradient. Using a small old blade repurposed from an old potato-digger and two two-by-eight planks, Grandpa and Uncle Wayne created an implement to dig the ditch for the water to run down.

To remove the water from the ditch, they initially used a spade to open the ditch to a certain depth. They cut several holes and left to give time for the water to run as far as it could. Upon returning they usually found a disaster because the cuts in the sandy ditch had either been sealed by a collapsing ditch or opened wide with all the water running down one or two rows. This method of water distribution would not work in these soil conditions.

After thought, they collected discarded wooden lathe. They cut them to the proper length and nailed four together forming a long rectangular box with a lid. They cut open the ditch, placed the wooden tube, and closed the ditch. The water ran evenly from the spouts and the problem was solved. It was laborious, but labor was available.

Later, the banker who refused to grant Grandpa a loan, became wealthy by making irrigation loans to all the other farmers in the valley who followed Grandpa's lead. Grandpa always enjoyed reminding him of that fact.

1951--Four Years Old

On December 19th, my little sister, Shelli, was born.

1952—Five Years Old

The Farm

One of Grandpa Beck's eighty-acre pieces of land was in a flat where water did not drain easily. Over the eons of time the standing water evaporated, but in so doing, brought salts from deeper in the soil and left them near the top of the ground. The soil became extremely salty. This destroyed the soil's structure and changed it from one in which water could easily flow through to a soil with an impermeable structure like concrete. Its tiny particles did not allow water to penetrate it, thus the water stood on top and eventually evaporated each time it rained. This made the soil ever-more alkaline, making it impossible to farm. Tractors frequently became stuck and needed another tractor to pull it out. Often, the second tractor became stuck. It was a mess.

It was partly due to this problem that Dad added the thirty-seven horsepower JD 60 to the twelve horsepower B's. He bought a single bladed chisel to pull behind the JD 60. He took the chisel to the alkaline farm. George took a JD B along with every log chain Dad owned and, when Dad became stuck, attached it to the front of the JD 60 and they were off. Dad dropped the chisel into the earth and the tractor began to spin its tires. That was when the B took up the slack in the chain and helped the JD 60 out of that hole. Sometimes George would become stuck, and Dad would have to carefully avoid also becoming stuck to pull George out. And so went the days until the farm was crisscrossed by the chisel.

The purpose of the chisel was to open the earth and facilitate the water to penetrate the soil and drain to the water table. In so doing, little by little, rains would carry away the excess salt in the soil that made the soil alkaline. It would take years to completely recover the soil. Dad, however, was not a patient man.

On the alkaline farm, there were five acres that had never been farmed because they were extremely alkaline. For this area, Dad bought a post-hole digger for the JD 60. He also crisscrossed this area by drilling a posthole every ten feet in all directions. He and George took Dad's old Dodge truck to a sand pit and filled it with sand and gravel. They returned to the postholes and, one by one, filled them by hand with sand and gravel, shoveling the sand and gravel into the holes. Each hole allowed water to drain below the alkaline level and, hopefully, would eventually reclaim an area with a five feet radius around each posthole. Today, this land is highly productive.

My First Plowing Experience

Dad always was trying to obtain more production from his resources. One spring he was plowing the cropland on the home quarter. He had two JD Bs and two plows, each with two fourteen-inch bottoms. This meant that each time through the field, each plow could plow a slice of soil twenty-eight inches wide. Dad had George performing another task and Dad was frustrated with only being able to plow a few acres each day.

That was when Dad had an idea. Leslie was seven years old, and I was five years old. In Dad's mind, we were old enough to drive a tractor. Dad hooked up the JD Bs to the two plows. He placed the tractor's right back tire in the furrow which was already made. He lowered the plow into the ground and turned over the driving to Leslie. All he had to do was to keep the back tractor tire in the fourteen-inch-wide furrow. Dad ran back and did the same thing to my plow. Once he had me going down Leslie's furrow, Dad jumped from my tractor and ran to overcome Leslie's tractor. When Leslie reached the end of the row, Dad had covered the distance between our plows. He jumped up onto the tractor, took the steering wheel from Leslie's hands and pulled the plow out of the ground. He then took it to where we would return to the other side of the field, dropped the plow into the ground and made sure the back-right tractor tire was in the furrow.

I grew nervous as Dad tended to Leslie's tractor and plow while my tractor was approaching the fence at the end of the field. I watched Dad finish with Leslie and then I looked at the shortening distance between me and the fence at the end of the row. Finally, Dad made it in time to turn my tractor. He always made it. Once or twice my tractor's wheel escaped the furrow and ran into the plowed ground. I fought to return it to the proper furrow. I was extremely nervous that it would happen again. I did not want Dad to be disappointed in me. I was not excited about doing it again. At the end of the day, Dad was exhausted. He was thirty-eight years old and happy with what we had accomplished. He must have been in excellent physical condition.

Chores

Leslie was seven years old, old enough to manage the automatic milking machines. Each machine weighed from fifteen to twenty pounds. First, he had to take a rag and dip it in warm water to wash each of the cows' tits. He threw a rubber strap over the cow and fastened it under the cow. To this strap, he reached in and lifted the milking machine to connect it to the strap. Then he connected each of the pulsating suction cups to each of the cows' tits.

We had two machines. Once he had the first machine connected, he had to complete the same process on a second cow. Then, he had to keep his eye on the first machine so that he could remove it when the machine had removed the cow's milk. This required concentration because not every cow took the same time to milk. He had to know about how long each cow took to milk so the machine would not be left on the cow too long.

My job was to place feed in each of the cow's places in the stanchion to encourage the cows to enter the barn and to give them essential nutrients that the grass did not provide. I kept the almost twenty cats away from the milk that was waiting to have its cream separated from the milk. As Leslie finished milking each cow, I opened the door to the barn and guided her outside.

When Leslie finished milking all the cows, he had the milk stored in a container on the cream separator. He started the electric motor and caught the cream in a nice clean container while the skim milk poured into an old bucket. When done, I took the cream to the house and poured it into the cream can. Leslie filled a couple cat dishes with skim milk and then took the rest to the hogs.

The hogs could smell the skim milk coming and they were all fighting for the best position at the front of the trough.

I also started the job of caring for the chickens.

Land Leveling

Wanting to increase his irrigated corn production, Dad hired a man with a Cat crawler with a push-fill scraper to level about twenty acres. The crawlers were slow moving and had trouble filling their scrapers with our sandy soils, but there was no one else leveling land, so Dad had to use this man if he were to have more irrigated land. The job was taking longer than predicted and becoming more expensive with each hour, then the scraper broke down and the man needed to drive to Omaha (two hours in each direction) to buy parts. He left the Cat running. He charged by the clock on the Cat, so he charged Dad full rates for moving dirt when the Cat did not move. That made the leveling project expensive. Dad was not happy and swore never to try that again.

Dad had a couple of irrigation ditches straightened. All the ditches on the quarter had the slope of the ditches changed to make it follow a more consistent gradient. The focus was to make the water run farther down rows in each direction from the ditch. Dad would be able to irrigate several more acres because of the leveling and with a consistent slope, irrigation would be easier.

The One Room Country School House

I had been wanting to go to school since the day Leslie started. Now, it was my turn, and I was not so sure anymore. I was scared. There were twenty-three children going to our one-room country school and I only knew Leslie.

I did not want to leave the car, but Mom was busy and had to return to her chores. Leslie grabbed my hand and walked me into the small schoolhouse. He took me to the back of the school where Mrs. Badge was talking to other students. Mrs. Badge looked at me and extended her hand for me to shake. I was having none of it, but she was nice. She led me to a desk and had one of the big boys adjust the desk height to fit my height.

When it was time to start school, she had one of the big kids pull the large rope to ring the bell. Children came from the swing set on the east side of the school and from the open area on the west side of the school and from the pasture across the road. Mrs. Badge assigned seats and the big boys adjusted each desk chair to fit the student. Then, she passed out the books from kindergarten to eighth grade. There were two other students with me in kindergarten: Linda Beck (no relation) and Janice Prososki.

She ordered all students to look at their books while she called the kindergarten class to the stage area in the back of the room. She introduced us to our books and spent time with us before returning us to our seats and calling the first-grade students.

Then we had recess. Everyone raced outside. Some students went to the swings while others crossed the graveled road, going down into the ditch and then up the other side. On the corner were wooden steps up and over the barbed wire fence leading into an overgrazed pasture full of milk cows. The big boys ran about to find pieces of old fence posts or old, dried cow patties. They placed one for home plate and then counted steps off for first, second, and third bases. Then, they chose up sides. Some of the boys had old baseball gloves, others had nothing. Someone produced a bat, and the game was on. The owner of the pasture and the cows did not mind if we left the cows alone and did not dig holes.

On the west side of the school, on the edge of the property was an old fallen cottonwood tree with a girth of at least three feet. It had a branch that someone had sawed off that was at least one foot in diameter. I liked to run there and pretend the main trunk was a horse and the sawed-off branch was the horse's neck. Other students also had a similar dream, so at the beginning of recess, we all ran fast to secure first place on the horse's back. We could not spend long on the trunk because we had to share. I was not a fan of sharing.

The girls and smaller children were playing ring-around-the-rosy. This was where I sometimes ended up. I did not like that game because it seemed like someone always chose me to be "it." I was not used to playing with other children and behaved badly.

Everyone enjoyed the swing set with its slide. The big boys would swing high and then bale out of the swing to see who could fly the farthest from the swing. More than one boy hit hard after falling off-balance. The little kids tried to emulate the big boys, but we were never as successful.

My school day ended at noon. Since Mom was terribly busy, I walked home every day. It was about one and a half miles. I was slow because I stopped to throw large pieces of gravel at fence posts, especially if there was a bird perched on it. It always took me a long time to reach home, but no one cared as long as I made it home safely. I always enjoyed the walk home.

Dad gave me a nickel for each time I walked home. I always looked forward to receiving my nickel. One day a farmer drove by in his pickup truck. He saw me and stopped and offered to give me a ride. I, wanting to receive my nickel, refused. He laughed and told me he would let me out by the cottonwood trees that marked the beginning of the farmstead. He assured me that no one would see me, and I could still receive my nickel. I climbed into his pickup. I have no idea which neighbor it was who offered me the ride. I am sure he told Dad the first time he saw him.

As time passed, I grew to love our country school. Since the teacher had to teach eight grades plus kindergarten, we never had much individual time with her, but we had other advantages. I loved to listen to the big kids' classes, especially science. While still in kindergarten, I knew that there were nine planets, and I could tell you all about them. I was a sponge listening to all the other kids' discussions with the teacher.

During recesses, we had all kinds of activities. Once we tried to build a sod house. On one corner of the property there was brome grass, which had a thick root system and made for excellent sod bricks. We managed to build three layers of sod before our interest moved elsewhere.

The little kids started to explore the culverts that ran under the cross-roads. We collected tall grass and used it to plug the ends of the culverts and then played hide-and-seek using the culverts as places to hide.

The big kids started trapping. A farmer agreed to teach them. Together they created a trap line, which they checked daily. Once they caught a skunk. The farmer taught them to remove the skin and stretch it to dry on the barn wall.

Once, in the spring, the big boys walked around raiding squirrels' nests. They found three baby squirrels and gave them to three members of the group. Leslie was in the group and was awarded one. He took it home and we fed it using doll bottles.

After recess, Mrs. Badge read from a book about cowboys. It settled everyone down. I loved this time and enjoyed all the cowboy books she read to us. I liked Mrs. Badge.

All students participated in the maintenance of the school. An older student swept the floor and moved the desks and then replaced them. I loved cleaning the erasers. To do this, we had to step outside. That was more difficult in the winter. In the mornings, a student took the drinking bucket outside to the hand pump and filled it with water. He returned it to its proper place in the hallway. The hallway was also the place where we placed our coats, boots and drinking cups. We used a dipper to fill our water cup. There was another bucket so that students could empty their cup without going outside if they did not drink it all.

The school had a multi-seat toilet outside for each gender. It was cold in the winter, but it served its purpose nicely. In the wintertime, no one wasted time before returning to the classroom. In the spring and fall, some students were known for lingering in the out-houses. Mrs. Badge would send a boy to bring back the lingerer. It was always the boys who lingered.

Sometimes our parents needed to communicate with us or we with them. That was a problem because the school had no telephone. We were fortunate to have the Walter Becks living next to the school... and they had a phone. Poor Mrs. Beck. She received so many messages from our parents and somehow was able to relay them on to our school. Mrs. Beck had a baby at home and could not easily take care of the baby and deliver a message. Often, Mrs. Badge had to leave a big kid in charge of the classroom while she ran over to call a student's parents. There were no answering machines at that time. If the person they were trying to call was not home, the teacher had to make multiple trips before she was able to talk with the parent. Communication was not easy.

In the winter, Mrs. Badge had to start the old oil furnace located in the back left-hand side of the building. We always opened all the doors on the furnace so that more heat would escape. When it snowed, we got our gloves wet. When we came in from recess, we always placed our wet gloves on the doors and on top of the furnace. We had to watch them carefully so they would not overheat and start a fire.

Sometimes I would come back early from recess or lunch and stay close to the furnace for extra heat. When the teacher started class and I had to leave my favored position by the furnace, I always felt cold for a few minutes. By the side of the furnace, there was a map of the world. I was impressed with how large Brazil, Russia, and China were. China and Russia worried me because we were in the middle of a cold war with them, mostly Russia. China did not have much technology, but Russia did.

The Squirrel

The little guy grew. He quickly started hopping around the house. We had to be careful where we stepped, because he would hop a few times and then stop. We had to be careful because he would climb under the covers on a bed, curl up, and sleep. We always had to check the covers before sitting on a bed. He slept in Dad's shirts that he hung on the back of a chair at bedtime. He climbed into the pocket and then curled up with his nose at the bottom of the pocket and covered it up with his tail. He was a little fur ball.

In the fall, he started collecting my sister, Shannon's doll blankets and tried to drag them up the side of the fireplace. He was making a nest on top of the fireplace mantel. He was so busy and worked so hard to take nest-worthy objects up to the mantel. Eventually, he had a nice nest to which he would retire to early every evening.

He loved to climb the curtains and run along the curtain rods. Occasionally, he jumped on someone's shoulder. He preferred tall people, like Mom and Dad. One day we received a visit from one of the town's ladies. She had no children, so she kept her house immaculate, and she dressed very fancy for our rural culture. She left her car, a Cadillac, knocked on the door and started climbing the steps to our kitchen. We opened the door and she stepped into the kitchen when, from the curtain rod jumped a furry animal and landed on her shoulder. She screamed, threw her hands up, although she managed to hang on to her fancy purse. She turned, jumped down the steps, rushed to her Cadillac and peeled out leaving rubber tracks on the driveway. She never called again. We felt bad.

The squirrel had refined tastes. You could line up six or more assorted brands of empty soda bottles on the counter and turn him lose. Every time he went to the 7-Up bottle and licked the top. You could also line up roses of every color and he would eat the red rose, every time.

It was fun giving him an ear of corn and watch him grab seeds and eat only the germ part of each seed. He was always focused. When done eating a kernel, he could spit it out flinging it great distances. When he sat on the counter, devouring an ear of corn, germless kernels were found in a six-foot radius. Mom was not pleased with his reach, but we were impressed.

As the squirrel grew older, we allowed him to play in a tree by the house. After a while, he always returned, and we took him inside the house and released him to play there. One day, we became distracted watching the squirrel as he played. When we looked for the squirrel, he was gone. We saw him from time to time, playing with another squirrel. We presumed it was a female and that he was now as happy as any squirrel could be.

Corn Incident with Shannon

Previously, during the fall corn harvest, Dad asked George to fill a shed with shelled corn in anticipation of the steers arrival within the next month. On this day, George placed an auger on the concrete platform so that it could receive the corn from the truck and carry it up and into the small storage shed.

As George started the process of emptying the truck, he busied himself with other tasks in the area. When the corn stopped flowing, he used the truck's hydraulic system to raise the front end of the truck box for more corn to flow. During this process, he lowered the back end of the truck. When the corn was again flowing, George started performing other tasks. That was when I decided that I would climb into the back of the truck and play in the corn. The corn flowing into a funnel that was the small door leading to the auger, created pressure, like standing in a fast-moving stream. There was a tendency for light objects to be knocked over. I was used to it and kept myself to one side, which was much safer. Then Shannon wanted up too. She reached up for me to pull her up. Not wanting to disappoint her, I helped her into the truck. She stood in the middle of the back end of the truck and directly in front of where the corn was flowing into the auger. That was when the corn shifted backward and pressed her against the back of the truck. She was almost covered up to her neck in corn. I did not know what to do. Then the force of the corn flowing through the narrow gate knocked her off her feet. Her face quickly disappeared under the corn. I started yelling feverishly to George while trying to keep Shannon's nose and mouth free so she could breathe. I was panicking as the moving corn dragged her deeper into the corn, making it more difficult for me to keep her nose and mouth free. That is when George appeared and quickly pulled her free from the corn. He held her tightly as she cried. He calmly asked me to get out of the truck. George was always calm. George was a good man.

Bootsy

I do not remember when Bootsy arrived. My first memories of the young black and white dog were of her following Dad everywhere. Dad had a Dodge pick-up that he had traded a side of beef for in the aftermath of World War II, when both vehicles and meat were scarce. The pickup had running boards and Bootsy always wanted to accompany Dad when he drove out of the yard. Most of the time that was fine, but there were a few times he did not want the dog with him. Bootsy followed Dad around the yard as he was leaving. When Dad was not looking, she jumped onto the running board, sat down, and stuck her head around the back of the cab to receive the effect of the wind passing by. Once or twice, when Dad turned to the right, caught her off-balance and she fell from the truck. Luckily, there was never any on-coming traffic. When Dad saw her peaking around the side of the pickup, he had to stop and let her into the cab where she was safe.

The Castor Oil Caper

Once Leslie and I were bored and wanted to receive some attention from Mom. We complained to her that we did not feel good and held our stomachs. After making the complaint a couple of times, our busy mother came over and felt our foreheads for our temperature. Obviously, we did not have a temperature. We were faking it. Then Mom asked Leslie if he had recently had a bowel movement. We had no idea what that was. Leslie took a stab in the dark and answered "no." Mom stood and went into the bathroom, opened a cabinet, and dug around. In the far back of the cabinet she found what she was looking for and pulled it out. She used her hand to smooth and clean the label. She returned to the kitchen to fetch a soup spoon. She poured the oily contents into the spoon and told Leslie to swallow. His reaction was not good. He almost gagged. He was a bit theatrical, but the downside was that the taste of the oily substance was not pleasant. He drank water, but that did not help. Mom turned to me with the spoon still firmly in her grip. She asked me if I had had a bowel movement recently. I answered "yes!" But guess what! Leslie had another surprise in a couple of hours. I felt sorry for him, but I still laughed. Now, we both knew what a bowel movement was.

Grandma's and Grandpa's Place

Grandma and Grandpa Tyler lived on the south side of the Platte River, close to the river. Their old house was located on the highest part of the farm and was surrounded by old trees. Hanging from a big, low branch was an outdated balance used to weigh watermelons. Grandpa loved to produce watermelons, which he sold from his yard during watermelon season. There was a normal wire gate used to enter the yard, except this one had a three-foot vertical extension which they used to prevent their Chocolate Labrador, Rex, from grabbing a hog head after butcher day and jumping over the gate into the yard with it, which he could do easily in his younger days. Grandma did not like hog heads on her front porch. Now, the metal gate was rusty, and the height extension had half fallen. It had not been needed in years since Rex was on the other side of youth and could only jump the gate with a hog head in his mouth in his dreams.

When we arrived, we never knocked. We opened the screen door to the porch and rushed to the next door, which led to the kitchen. Grandma was usually scurrying about the kitchen. She always smiled when we burst in, and she came to meet us to give us a hug. The kitchen always smelled of things baking in the oven and the coffee pot was always on. She was responsible for baking the turkey and bread roles, which she always heated the woodburning stove with corn cobs. Both the turkey and bread roles were delightful. When we asked her what her secret was, she always replied that it was the corn cobs. She had a gas stove but did not use it except to heat water for coffee and other such things.

Grandpa was around the corner in the dining room sitting in his easy chair, often taking a nap. By his side, also sleeping, was Rex, who was old, deaf, and suffering from arthritis. He was protective of Grandpa. We had to slow down and give Rex a wide birth to approach Grandpa from the other side to avoid Rex's wrath. Grandpa did not say much, but he was the center of the family. Everyone who came in greeted Grandpa Tyler.

On our family gatherings, Uncle Wayne and Aunt Lucille came with their three children: Kathy, Dan, and Brian. Kathy was one year older than me, while Dan was two years younger. Brian was about five years younger than me. There was Uncle Joe, who was Leslie's age, and Uncle Paul and Aunt Jean with their three children, all of whom were much younger than I was.

When we arrived, everyone placed their coats in Grandpa's and Grandma's room and then the commotion started. Kids were running every which way. Grandma had placed a card table just behind Grandpa's chair, but still in the kitchen. On it were a bottle of Canadian Club with bottles of Squirt and 7-Up to make whiskey sours and whiskey sweets. Ice with tongs were also there. When everyone arrived, Grandpa, Dad, Wayne, and Paul made themselves their favorite drinks. We were too young to participate.

Talks inevitably moved from crops to prices of corn and pork. Uncle Wayne was starting to increase the size of his pork production.

They also talked about hunting. Grandpa and my uncles loved to hunt ducks, geese, deer, pheasant, and quail. They were good hunters, demanding that everyone follow safety protocol. Once we young ones reached ten years of age, they allowed us to accompany the adults on the hunts; although, we were each tightly supervised. Dad did not hunt. He said that when he saw an animal, he would rather take a photograph of it than to kill it, but he did not stop Leslie and me from hunting; although, I cannot remember killing any birds. My aim was always off.

For Thanksgiving and Christmas, we ate two huge turkeys which Uncle Wayne carved. He stood and held the knife and the sharpener and ran them back across each other to sharpen it. He did this while carrying on a conversation. Before he carved the turkey, he or Grandma offered a prayer. Then he carved the turkey and passed plates of turkey around. The table had everything from mashed potatoes to sweet potatoes to macaroni and corn, turkey stuffing and a host of other goodies. It was fabulous.

Since not everyone could sit at the main table, there was a kid's table. There were a multitude of young kids that were too young to sit at the main table. It was always a privilege to be asked to join the adults at the main table.

I remember the taste of Grandpa's and Grandma's water was different. It seemed sweeter. I could not put my finger on how it was different, but I always associated it with their house and the Platte River.

We always had to leave the party early because we had to go home, change clothes, and then milk the cows, care for the chickens, feed the hogs and the fat cattle. It was dark before we finished and went inside. I resented the milk cows because I did not want to leave the party early and some days it would have felt good not to be cold even once, but we had to milk the cows no matter what the weather conditions.

Our Christmas Celebration

Christmas was special. We all made lists of what we wanted, and I was always specific in what I wanted and expected to receive it. I was very spoiled and mostly unappreciative. I do not know how I got to be that way, but I was. We cousins exchanged names, plus we could expect presents from each pair of aunts and uncles. Of course, we expected our largest present from Mom and Dad.

Grandma always had a beautiful cedar tree cut from the pasture and wonderfully decorated. She used colorful lights looked like they had long candles emitting from a socket on each tree branch. It was so soothing to sit and watch the candles. They seemed like they were rotating. Under the tree were presents from all his hunting buddies from Omaha and Lincoln. They usually sent boxes of chocolate to show appreciation for their being allowed to hunt on the river.

Christmas eve arrived early, and we went to Grandpa's and Grandma's house early in the evening and unloaded all the presents from the car. Some, I had seen under our tree and some I had never seen before. We boys had to help unload the car and put the packages under the tree, or close to it. If uncles Wayne and Paul had not arrived, more packages would be added to the tree. The excitement was off the charts. I know I was bouncing off the walls. In a couple of hours, we would open the packages, and I would know what I received.

First, Dad, the uncles and Grandpa had to have their Canadian Club sweets or sours and the women were setting the table for a light lunch. Mom, the aunts, and Grandma were rushing from the kitchen to the table to set the table.

Grandpa made the table from walnut trees that he had cut on the farm. Grandpa made an expandible table. All he had to do was to make another leaf and add it to the others. Every time a child was born, he created a new leaf and added it to the table, and Grandpa invited another one of us to leave the children's table and eat with the adults at the big table.

We ate quickly and tried to hurry the men and women. The men were still sipping on their Canadian Clubs and the women were clearing the table and doing the dishes. Then everyone that could, found a place to sit or kneel around the tree. There were so many presents that it was impossible to hand them out one by one. We had two or three people handing out presents. Everyone was ripping them open and casting the torn wrappings everywhere.

Mom was uncomfortable with all the senseless waste. She wanted people to open their presents sensibly so that the paper could be reused next year. She was a child of the depression, and they never forget all those years they were deprived of things, things that were now abundant. I can only imagine her disappointment in me because of my selfishness and sense of entitlement that I had. Years later, I served two tours in the Peace Corps and grew accustomed to living a very modest life where my income was severely limited and I still had more than most people had, so I can understand what she felt. Today, I wash dishes in a restaurant. The quantity of food that people return uneaten on plates is enormous. I know that today in most countries thousands of people would fight to eat the food collected in my sink. I think of that every day.

As we opened more presents, everyone was commenting about their presents and about others' presents. No one could understand anything the volume was so loud. Soon, after we had opened all presents, each family made a pile of gifts that we needed to load into our cars. Mom salvaged what wrapping paper was not damaged too extensively, and the rest was discarded for burning in the furnace. We said goodbye, loaded our vehicles and headed home.

On Christmas day, we again gathered at Grandpa and Grandma Tyler's house for a special dinner. This day was like Thanksgiving. Grandma made the bread and the turkey and Mom, and the aunts made all the side dishes. The men made their Canadian Club drinks and the kids bounced off the walls by running around and shouting. It was just this side of chaos.

At some point, we gathered at the table, Grandma or Uncle Wayne said a prayer, the turkey was carved, and the eating began. There was joking, and everyone was included in the conversation, except for Grandpa. He was quiet but listening to everything and laughing often. Grandpa was a quiet person.

1953 (6 years old)

Sheri Was Born

On August 3rd, 1953, Mom had a busy day. She separated the dirty clothes into a dozen piles before running each pile through the washing machine. She then placed each article of clothing between two hot rollers to remove as much water as possible. She had to be careful because if her hand were caught in the machine, it could burn her or break a bone in her arm. Then she grabbed a rag and went outside to the clothesline. She ran the rag up and down the four wires used to dry the clothes outside. Her purpose was to clean them so the wires would not dirty the clean clothes.

Mid-morning, Mom started cooking dinner for the family and the hired men. After dinner, she had to do dishes and clean the kitchen. That done, she went to the garden and picked several bushels of sweetcorn. She took the corn under a shade tree and husked each ear. She removed the kernels from the cobbs with a knife and canned dozens of quarts of sweetcorn.

Then it was chore time. She was milking the twelve cows that we had when, with one cow remaining, she went into labor. She caught George who was on his way to his truck at 6:00 p.m. He called Dr. Douglas who took Mom to the Central City hospital. George finished the chores and made the four of us kids supper while he kept us entertained. Dad came home from the field eventually and rushed to the hospital. There had been no way to send a message to him because George did not want to leave us kids alone. Sherilyn Joy Beck was born at 6:48 p.m.

Putting Up Hay

Putting up hay was the process of taking hay that we already had cut, dried, windrowed, and gathered it into bunches with either the loader or a sweep. The sweep, if there was one, would go about the field and follow the windrowed hay and gather it into a bunch.

The sweep then took it near the haystack that we were forming and deposited it for the loader to easily collect it. The loader, if no sweep was present, would gather the hay. Once gathered, the driver approached the haystack from the position that would allow him to fill the lowest spot on the stack. It was his job to frame the stack. On top of the stack were one or two men with pitch forks. It was their job to walk around the hay and compact it as much as they could. They also fine-tuned the placement of the hay. They gave the stack the familiar bread-loaf shape.

Usually, it was brutal physical work to be the stacker. Walking around a stack while you sank into the hay up to your knees or waist, and then pulled hay this way or that way to give the stack even lines, was very tiring. While doing this, they had to stay out of the way of the loader because the loader driver's vision was impeded by the load of hay on his loader. It was possible to stab a stacker with a sharp tooth in the loader's array of teeth. It was also possible to drop the loader on top of the stackers or knock a stacker from the stack. Both the stackers and the driver had to be careful. The driver had to approach the stack slowly and deliberately. Safety had to always be a consideration.

George usually mowed the hay and raked it. Leslie, at seven years old, drove the loader. Dad and George were on top of the stack. Dad allowed me to rake scatterings. Scatterings were small bunches of hay that escaped the sweep or loader. They needed to be collected to avoid their interfering with the next mowing by plugging the mower. The scattering rake was a straight dump rake. It was incredibly old. I am certain horses first pulled it when it was new. I took pride in keeping the scatterings collected and deposited near the stack so Leslie could easily load them onto his loader. Sometimes I struggled, from lack of strength in my arms, in triggering the rake to dump its load.

The loader consisted of a 1934 John Deere Model A with twenty-six horsepower. This tractor's only use on the farm was to put-up-hay. The sweep head placed on a loader could elevate the load of hay to a maximum of fifteen feet. The JD A was not difficult for a man to steer, but less friendly for a young person. In addition, the placement the weight of the hay on the loader, which was carried in front of the tractor, put much weight on the front wheels making it much more difficult to steer. It was a miracle that Leslie could manage to drive it.

Dad allowed Leslie to drive the JD A because he could. Somehow, he made it work. Leslie knew that if he loaded the hay from the line of raked hay a certain way, it would be easier for the stackers to dislodge pitchforks of hay to landscape the top of the stack. Many drivers were not aware of this and collected the hay from the lines of swept hay in a way that tied the hay into knots, making untangling the knots a major task. It made the stackers job much more difficult, and it was already difficult. That is why Dad placed Leslie on the loader. Leslie was careful and deliberate on the loader. He always placed his load perpendicular to the stack before elevating the load. He knew that it was very dangerous to start elevating the load while still turning to approach the stack. Once in position, he elevated the load to as much as fifteen feet. Then he drove a few feet to place the load on the stack. Driving the JD A with that much weight on the front wheels was difficult and dangerous.

Shannon and the Elevator Spring Caper

Shannon was four years old and exploring the yard with all its machinery. As luck would have it, the ear corn elevator was in operation. Dad had modernized the operation by replacing the JD B and its PTO system with an electric motor taken from an irrigation well. The elevator had an eight-foot dragline piece at the end that we lifted before we pulled the wagon in. Then we dropped the piece to the ground and the wagon backed up a foot or two to place it in position to unload the ear corn into the elevator dragline.

The dragline was heavy, but it had to be light enough for a ten-year old boy to lift because they were usually the ones bringing the loaded wagons. To overcome this problem, two large springs were placed on the dragline, one on each side. When the ten-year-old lifted, the springs would lift most of the weight. When the dragline was beyond center of gravity, gravity was holding it in place and the springs were lose because they held no weight. Sometimes the springs fell on the outside of the elevator and sometimes they fell inside the elevator. On this day, they rested on the inside of the elevator.

Shannon saw the elevator and found it interesting. She was attracted to the board that held the start and stop buttons for the electric motor. She looked long and hard at the buttons and pushed the green one. The elevator sprang into action with the springs inside the elevator frame. A spring caught on a paddle and was stretched. It gave way and was jettisoned forward, narrowly missing Shannon. It was headed to the top of the elevator when George came and pressed the red button, stopping the elevator. He climbed the elevator and retrieved the destroyed spring. Then he grabbed Shannon's hand and walked her back to the house and Mom. George was always there to save us.

Doc Douglas

We were usually healthy, but sometimes we needed a vaccination or help with a cold or the flu. It was then that we visited Doc Douglas. He was an old man, already with white hair. His office was on the corner across the street from the library and on the first floor. As one would expect, it smelled of a doctor's office. He had a waiting room with stained oak furniture with a nice red upholstered soft covering on every piece. I remember the constant tick-tock of an old clock placed above the waiting room bench. There was usually someone besides us there waiting.

When we entered his inner office, he took our temperature and had us cough, depressed our tongue and looked inside our mouth, then he took our blood pressure. I did not like it when it was time for a shot. His needles were not sharp. He kept his stash of needles, all sizes, and varieties, in a small steel container. He reached in and selected a needle and gave us the shot. It always hurt because he did not sharpen his needles very often. For sterilization, he may have poured boiling water over them. I am not sure what precautions he took. I was too young to know.

Doc still made house calls on older and sickly patients. He was a much-appreciated member of the community.

Doc Shaw

Not only did my hometown have a doctor, but it also had a dentist. Doc Shaw was also an older man with white hair and moustache. His office was upstairs from Doc Douglas' office. We walked upstairs, always reluctantly, because the dentist's work always hurt—a lot. I cannot remember specifically, but he gave a shot for pain. If so, he used reusable needles that seemed very dull.

A pulley powered his drill connected to a foot pedal. The faster he pumped, the faster the drill bit spun. He had to keep the drill spinning while holding a mirror and doing the drilling. It was not an exact science. And it hurt. I always squirmed making the Doc's job even more difficult. He had no assistants to help him. He had a round spittoon bowl nearby. It had water circulating in it. We often had to spit into the spittoon to get rid of excess saliva and blood that had built up in our mouths.

The Wagon Incident with Shannon

On a fall's sunny day, four-year-old Shannon was outside exploring. She was by the old machine shed by the house and found an empty wagon. Wagons at that time were small and used regular vehicle tires. Curious what was in the wagon, she found a way to climb on top of the tire. She was reaching to grab something to climb even higher when the wagon moved. Someone had hooked a tractor to the empty wagon and was in the process of moving it. The turning tire threw her forward, to the ground, and passed over her. As luck would have it, she was scared, but unhurt. Shannon was a lucky little girl. Mom took her to see Dr. Douglas.

Saturday Night

Saturday night was a special night. We all took baths and dressed up, not in a Sunday-go-to-church suit, but new and clean clothes. It was difficult to find parking on the main block. We often had to park around the corner. The town had three grocery stores. Mom had her favorite where she stocked up for the following week. She did this towards the end of the night so that things that needed refrigeration would not have time to warm up too much.

Once a month we all went to the barber shop. Farmers and their children packed it. It was an open forum for discussion of timely topics. I sat in a chair and looked at hunting and car magazines. Dad never joined the discussions. He preferred to keep his opinions to himself; although, the barber loved to talk, which increased the time needed to complete each haircut. He always stopped cutting hair to make a point and he waved his hands when he did. I was impatient because I wanted to get my haircut so I could walk both sides of our busy main street.

Clarks also had a movie theater, a hardware store, a five-and-dime, and a cooperative operated store. I liked to walk the block, cross the street, and walk back. If I walked slowly, it could take ten minutes. I loved walking by the theater where I heard loud bangs and booms if it was a war movie. I did not know anyone, but I did not mind walking alone. In front of the hardware store there was even a popcorn machine.

Every store had its doors open and people were everywhere inside the store and around the entryway. It was hard to enter or leave the stores because farmers or their wives were conversing with other farmers and their wives. There was a sense of excitement in the air. People were happy.

The stores closed soon after the movie finished. Sometimes people went to the movies and then made their purchases, especially their groceries. When the movie finished, a crowd of people burst into the street. Some people walked directly to their cars while others hurried to shop for groceries. They did not want to buy groceries before the movie started because they might have perishable items.

The Sow Stampede

It was a sweltering summer. I had to be at least six years old, but no more than eight. It was a summer where I did not have much responsibility, yet. On our farm we had milk cows, pigs, and chickens and about every kind of animal. But, on this day, in the early evening or the late afternoon, my mother had finished milking because she was still responsible for that when Leslie was on a tractor, and I was still too young to help much.

How this started is unclear. What happened after it started is clear. My mother was rushing around the barnyard finishing the details from milking. Mom never walked, she double-timed it because she was always in a hurry. The hired man, George, was near so it had to be before 6:00 o'clock. He worked hard all day, but his schedule never varied. At 7:00 o'clock in the morning, he arrived and at 6:00 p.m. he left. He was parking his equipment or walking towards his pickup when the ruckus started.

I was always very dirty because I played in the dirt constantly. I was barefoot and infatuated with a short rope that I had found somewhere. I was always exploring the buildings, the machinery, the sheds, the hayloft, and I was always finding interesting things. Anyway, the rope I found was about eight feet long. I was walking around trying to lasso everything like the cowboys did in the movies. I went to the cattle tank and tried to lasso fence posts and the waterspout, which carried water from the windmill to the tank. I also tried to lasso cows. The cows never reacted beyond flicking their tails disapprovingly. They looked at me, chewed their cud, and when I tossed the lasso, if it came close to their head; they tossed their head in a circular motion and the lasso missed. It always missed. I was tiring of missing my target.

Standing near the cow was a huge sow. She had her head down as she rooted the ground, tossing the dirt about, and always finding something to eat. She seemed an easier target, so I tried to lasso her. She was as tall as I was and weighed more than two hundred pounds. She did not run, but if I became too much of a bother, she would squeal in protest and take a few steps before stopping to root again. That reaction interested me, so I approached her again. As long as I did not cast my rope, she continued to ignore me, but I was tired of missing my target. I stepped back and viewed her from front to back. I saw the problem. It was impossible to rope her because she had no neck, and her head was always stretched downward toward the ground. There was no way for anyone to slip a rope around her neck, not even a cowboy could do that.

Again, I ran my eyes from her nose on the ground to her head, neck, body, and finally, sticking straight up; I saw it: her curly tail. Then I had an idea that would overcome all obstacles. It was perfect and simple. I walked up behind her while drawing the loop smaller and smaller. It was a brilliant idea. I smiled to myself in anticipation of my victory, and I slipped the rope onto her tail and gave it a snap to draw it tight.

What happened next was not in my plan. She bolted, trying to escape the rope on her tail. For some reason that even today I do not understand, my hands clenched the rope so tight that I became an extension of the rope. The hog squealed at the top of its voice, and I hollered at the top of my voice. The hog made a couple of small circles inside the corral, which at least was soft. All the manure was dry from the summer heat and was soft as a pillow.

The hog was not accustomed to having anything hanging onto its tail and it ran faster and faster trying to ditch me. It widened its circles and the centrifugal force almost cast me aside, but I hung on. I was not used to having anyone pull me around that I could not yell to stop, and they would. This hog would not listen to me, and I would not relax my grip. I did; however, continue to yell at the top of my lungs.

My mother heard me first. She ran to see what the fuss was and when she saw me bouncing on my behind as I was being pulled by a mad, run-away sow, she did the first thing that she could think of--she also yelled. At first the sow dragged me on my belly, but somehow, I managed to sit upright. She pointed her nose towards the open corral gate and increased her speed.

Mom continued to yell as she ran after the sow. George heard the commotion and entered the fracas; although, I doubt that he understood what was happening. As he caught up with Mom in the barn yard, Mom pointed toward where I was yelling, and he was now running ahead of Mom.

The hog entered the cattle lane, which led from the barn yard to the pasture and fields. It was wide enough for six or eight cows to walk side by side from the corral to the pasture. The only problem was that in about fifty feet there had been a huge mud hole, which always filled with water every time it rained. The hogs used it to cool themselves in hot weather. They covered themselves with mud and then, when comfortable, they would wonder off carrying several pounds of dirt. Over time, the hole became larger and larger. On the far side of the mud hole the ground level increased by at least a foot. It was like a giant step in the cattle lane, or the side of the Grand Canyon, depending on how you looked at it.

George was yelling for me to let go of the rope. I assume my mother was yelling the same thing. Both George and Mom were panting as I headed towards the muddy waters. As we drew closer, some hogs stood up to see what the commotion was and quickly took steps to vacate the central part of the lane, which my sow had chosen as her path. We hit the mud hole at full speed. The sow showed no sign of tiring or slowing down. Several startled hogs joined the squealing and joined the hog stampede towards the pasture. Mom and George were falling farther behind, at least before the sow jumped over the solid vertical ridge that marked the end of the mud hole. My bottom hit the ridge at full speed and that jolted me enough to force me to release my hold on the rope. With no resistance on the rope, the sow increased her speed and quickly rounded the corner and disappeared into the pasture.

Within seconds George and my mother caught up to me and checked me over for damages. They were not saying much because they were still catching their breath. Once she saw that I was no worse for the wear, she started giving me advice, let us call it advice anyway. She was frightened but also aggravated that I would consider doing such a thing. She did not understand that I never considered it. I just did it. If I would have considered it, I would not have done it. Nonetheless, with each step her grip on my arm tightened. If I had any chance of escape, I would have bolted just as the sow had down when I tightened the rope around its tail. I was trapped and had to accept whatever came, and it was coming.

George followed the sow. He had to remove the rope from her tail because it was tight enough to cut off the blood circulation. She was loose in a twenty-acre pasture and spooked. I fear that it took him awhile to calm her enough that she would allow him to loosen the rope, but George always accomplished the difficult tasks, and this would be no exception. George was always there when a crisis occurred.

1954 (7 years old)

Land Leveling

Dad wanted to produce more corn. Financially, he was unable to buy more farmland; therefore, he decided to make the existing land more productive. He wanted to level more land but did not trust other men to do it for him. They were expensive and unreliable. In one of his farm magazines, he saw an advertisement by Hancock scrapers located in Lubbock, Texas. Farm tractors could pull the scrapers behind them, and they should work easily in sand because the scraper used paddles to pull the dirt into the bucket. Dad called the number and negotiated for a five-yard scraper. It would be the first such scraper in the state of Nebraska.

He started looking for a tractor to pull it. He negotiated for an Oliver 88 tractor, which had thirty-seven horsepower, enough to pull the five-yard scraper. As part of the tractor deal, the dealership offered to pay for half of the fuel costs for thirty days. Later, this would come back to bite him.

They delivered the tractor just after wheat harvest. None of the neighbors paid attention, but later when Dad pulled into the yard with a huge yellow Hancock leveler on the back of his truck, they all noticed. Dad wanted to be discrete, so he hooked up the Oliver to the Hancock five yard and headed across a field to the backside of a shelterbelt to the wheat stubble. He wanted to adjust the machine to local conditions without anyone observing him.

Once behind the shelterbelt, Dad slowly lowered the bit and started the paddles moving. I am not sure what the problem was, but it was not working. Suddenly a neighbor came in his pickup and parked a safe distance from where Dad and George were working. Within minutes another two neighbors came and parked beside the first. They started conversing. I was bored and wandered among them and then over by Dad and back again. They paid no attention to me and spoke freely among themselves. Dad and George worked on the machine for more than two hours. The neighbors were sure it would not work and mentioned how foolish Dad was. Eventually, they gave up and left… somehow satisfied.

Shortly after the neighbors left, Dad was able to fill the scraper to the brim and he turned and dumped the dirt in a low area. It was working. Dad had surveyed the wheat stubble and he placed the cut and fill markers every one-hundred foot. The next day, Dad was in the field, cutting and filling and slowly moving across the field. Dad's work was rough, but he was learning how to use the machine. When he came in for dinner and supper, he was happy and proud. He knew that before he planted next year's crop, he would have every inch of the home-quarter leveled. Granted, he still used the existing irrigation ditches that ran through the fields. Labor used on irrigation would not necessarily be saved. He worked on the ditches to make their slope more consistent. That made irrigation easier, but we still had center ditches that required lots of walking to complete the irrigation process. This would be a major improvement, but there would still be room for more improvement in the future.

During the day, the Oliver 88 pulled the scraper, which was demanding work for the tractor. It consumed much diesel fuel. When the hired man went home, Dad unhooked the tractor and took it to an irrigation well that did not have an electric motor. It was powered by a tractor pulley. They unhooked the JD B from the pump and hooked up the Oliver. They did this every day for thirty days. When Dad presented the man at the dealership with the fuel bill, he nearly fell over. It was huge. Dad told him how many hours the tractor already had on its clock and the dealer could not believe it. It was more than most farmers put on a tractor in a year. Dad was happy. The dealer, not so much.

After the corn was harvested, Dad finished leveling his home quarter. Neighbors started going to him and asking him to level their land. Dad figured out how to charge and took on jobs. Dad was too busy to operate the machine as was George. Leslie could operate it, but during the fall and spring he could only work on Saturdays and after school. During the summer he could work every day. In fact, he did all the work on the first few farms that Dad leveled. I envied him and wanted to do it too.

Eventually, Dad found a dependable man and paid him to operate the scraper. Dad only charged for the machine when it was moving dirt. If the tractor became stuck, Dad did not charge the farmer for the time it took to pull it out. If the tractor driver was maintaining the tractor or scraper, Dad did not charge the farmer. In fact, if the driver stopped three times to relieve himself, he was expected to deduct fifteen minutes from his "machine hours."

During this time, I learned how to drive the Killefer and float. The Killefer was a blade used to smooth the cuts and fills that the scrapers made. The scrapers left the area very uneven and made it difficult to see where they should be cutting and filling. My job was to keep all the 100-foot lanes smooth.

The float also was a blade but placed on a long frame that did a better job at overall smoothness. Dad used the float after the scrapers had left the field. I started in one corner and worked the field on an angle. Then, I crisscrossed the field perpendicular from the original angle. By the time I finished, the field looked like a cutting board. When it rained, there would be no puddles, or Dad would return and fix it without charge. That happened very seldom.

Threshing Oats

This year my Grandpa Beck had many acres of oats. I do not remember why Dad did not combine them, but they instead used a thresher. This was a stationary machine that did the work of a combine, except that we had to take the crop to it. Dad contracted a man to bring his thresher, and another man to cut the oats and pull them into small bundles and tie a string around them.

The process required many men. Besides the thresher and cutter, there had to be a tractor driver pulling a hay wagon onto which three or four men with pitch forks were grabbing the small bundles of oats on each side of the wagon and piling them onto the wagon. There had to be two wagons because one was loaded while the other was unloaded.

Leslie and I drove the two wagons. It took men to unload the wagon, slice away the string that bound each bundle and throw the oats into the thresher. Another man had to manage the oat grain coming out of the thresher so that no truck or wagon spilled grain. Each truck and wagon had a driver. And it was hot with no breeze anywhere. The men were in danger of overheating.

At noon, everyone went to Grandma Beck's house for food. Several women had prepared different plates of meat, potatoes, vegetables, and pies. Food was very abundant because the women wanted the men to go home and praise the food they had had for lunch to their wives. Also, about four o'clock, Mom and Grandma brought iced tea and pie as a lunch. The men were hot and needed a rest. Eventually, the work was done, and everyone went home. It was a very labor-intensive job. The number of man-hours needed to harvest this would be considered unthinkable today.

Farming was still labor intensive. That is why most quarters had a homestead with a family living in it. That is why Saturday nights in town were so full of people and our schools were full. Much of our country's population was still rural.

First Television Set

Several neighbors had purchased a new black and white television set, including Grandma and Grandpa Beck. One day we came home from school and found a new set in the living room. It was glorious. We could receive reception on three channels: ABC, NBC, and CBS. My favorite shows included: Roy Rogers, Hopalong Cassidy, and The Lone Ranger. I could not watch them often because they had the 5:30 p.m. time slot and that was in the middle of chores. Reception was not always good.

Shannon Falls from Wagon Wheel

Shannon was five years old and was on one of her exploratory missions in the farmyard. She saw an empty wagon parked in front of the old shop, near the house. She found it interesting and approached it quickly. She climbed onto the back right tire which was the one facing the house. She was trying to climb higher when the wagon lurched forward, casting her forward. Whoever had hooked a tractor to the wagon had not looked around the wagon. She fell to the ground and the unloaded wagon passed over her small body. George was nearby and heard her scream. He rushed to her and checked her out. She was all right; except she was frightened. He walked her to the house and turned her over to Mom.

1955 (eight years old, third grade)

Going To Lubbock, Texas for Scraper Parts

Dad bought the first Hancock scraper in Nebraska from Mr. Hancock when Mr. Hancock was just starting his business. Mr. Hancock was grateful for Dad's introducing his scraper to Nebraska irrigation territory. Dad quickly learned what scraper parts would wear out. He could not afford to have scrapers stopped for lack of a small part. For this reason, Dad made a trip once or twice a year to Lubbock to buy parts, which he had shipped back to Nebraska. He even had the scraper drivers keep the parts most likely to break in their work pickups so that, if a scraper broke down, they could drive the pickup to the scraper and find the parts needed to repair it and quickly be back to work.

Once, Dad decided to take the family with him on a part run to Lubbock. He thought it would be good to introduce use to the states of Kansas, Oklahoma, and Texas. He also wanted us to see the big Hancock factory. Upon arriving, Dad walked into Mr. Hancock's office, and they talked general business. Dad was curious what Mr. Hancock was developing and Mr. Hancock was curious how his equipment was operating in the field. After that, they got down to business and ordered the parts. Of course, Mr. Hancock tried to sell Dad another scraper. In fact, he had a new thirty-three-yard self-propelled scraper that he wanted Dad to evaluate. Dad signaled Leslie to try it out. For one hour, Leslie drove back and forth loading and unloading that gigantic scraper. Leslie was ten years old. Dad was in the market for another scraper, but not one that large. He did buy an eight-yard scraper.

As for me, I could not believe how large a factory Mr. Hancock had. The ceilings were high. Cranes that picked up gigantic bars of steel and moved them from one place to another filled the area. Men were everywhere, yet they knew what to do. It was like an ant colony. Each man had a purpose.

With all business concluded, we returned to the motel to collect our things. We had a room on the second floor of the motel. We were all down by the car, except for Mom and two-year-old Sheri. That is when Sheri decided to stick her head between the iron bars on the railing that surrounded the outside of the walkway. Of course, she could not get it out. She was stuck and started to cry. Several other people who were also checking out heard her and came to watch. Dad rushed upstairs and tried to remove her head. Mom helped, but to no avail. The motel manager came and tried to help. Finally, the manager produced a bar with which Dad was able to separate the bars enough to release Sheri's head. All was well again, except for the stretched bars.

At home again, Dad visited the Oliver dealer and bought an Oliver 99 with eighty horsepower to pull the new eight-yard scraper. The dealer did not offer to pay for half of the fuel costs for the first thirty days. That deal was never again on the table.

1956 (nine years old, fourth grade)

Land Leveling

Dad's land leveling business was keeping him busy. In fact, he ordered an eight-yard scraper and a JD 820. This tractor was low to the ground and very clumsy. The big tractor was heavy and had wide tires, both good for better traction. The JD 820 only had thirty-two horsepower, but it could pull a big load due to its weight and wide tires. Everything about the JD 820 was inconvenient. It had a small gasoline engine that had to be started for it to start the diesel engine. If the gasoline engine would not start, it was impossible to start the diesel engine. The operator needed to ensure that he always had gasoline with him to keep the fuel tank supplied with gasoline for the starter engine.

Dad had learned to survey fields and was able to make maps showing how much to cut or fill at every 100-foot flag. He was dedicating more time to land leveling relative to farming. He had to visit farms in advance to flag and survey the land. He often used Leslie, Shannon, and me for this. We carried small plastic flags with a stiff wire shaft to push into the ground, and a survey rod made from a one by four board ten feet long. Finding that size rod too heavy for Shannon (only seven years old), Dad cut two feet off one rod for her.

After surveying, Dad made a map based on the instrument reading taken at each wire flag station. From this map, he calculated how much to cut or fill at each flag to achieve about a one-tenth of a percent gradient. For every one hundred feet, the gradient would decrease by one-tenth of a foot. Of course, some fields with a more severe natural slope had a steeper gradient and water would run faster. The one- to two-tenths of a foot slope per one hundred feet distance was optimal for irrigation. Greater slope could encourage erosion and did not soak into the soil as easily.

Next, we went to the field with wooden lathe. Dad drove down each row of flags. If there was a fill, the amount of that fill was written on the stake using a blue crayon. If there was a cut, the amount of the cut was written on the stake using a red crayon. Dad would drive the truck and write the amount on each stake. I, or Leslie, would get out of the truck and pound in the stake by the flag. We had to hurry because Dad was always in a hurry. If we were a little slow, Dad would take off without us and we had to run to catch up.

Often the soil was soft because the field had been disked or plowed. Driving through the field could cause the truck to overheat or otherwise stressed the engine. Other times, the field would contain tall weeds or grass. Dad would have the farmer shred the field. When Dad drove through the field, the truck's radiator would often become plugged, or partially plugged, causing the truck to overheat. This job caused pickups to age quickly.

Irrigation

With Dad spending more time with the land leveling enterprise, the irrigation fell to Mom and me. Dad assigned Leslie to driving a scraper. But irrigation had become easier to make sets. The ditches mostly had an even slope and that made it easier to maintain a ditch at a given level because there was only a one-tenth of a percent slope in the ditch.

Another improvement was that we now used siphon tubes instead of digging holes in the ditch. We had two types of siphons: rubber and plastic. The rubber tubes were flimsy, making them hard to set (get water flowing through them) and hard to carry. It was like carrying wet noodles. I only remember two-inch tubes. Later, we would be using at least a half dozen varied sizes depending on how long the rows were. We had rows that were no more than the length of a football field while others were one-half mile. We had ways of slowing down the water flow if the set were shorter than normal, requiring less water flow. Likewise, we could speed the flow if the set were longer and needed a faster flow.

The problem with these siphons was that they easily developed small holes in them, which could stop the flow of water. We often returned to make a set to find that tubes had stopped. With fewer tubes pulling water from the ditch, the water level climbed in the ditch, the remaining tubes, to some degree, could increase their flows. This may have been enough to compensate for the less water flowing out of the ditch from the stopped tubes. If not, there would be a ditch break and we would have to fix it, which was always difficult when the soil was very sandy. When we had made the repairs; we restarted the tubes. We stayed looking to isolate the tubes sucking air. If we found them, we had to look for the hole. Once found, we made a mud pie over them to seal them. This was a constant battle.

The plastic tubes were made from a thicker, transparent plastic. They were easier to start but they also suffered from holes. With these tubes, however, any tube sucking air would have an air bubble form in the top of the tube. Usually, close observation revealed the source of the air, and we could use a mud pie to make the repair.

A problem that remained was to identify each row that had the water reach the end of the row. To solve this problem, Dad decided to count every twenty rows and place a red flag. For the next twenty rows, he placed two red flags. When we reached fifth-twenty rows, we placed a blue flag. For the sixth-twenty rows, we placed a blue and a red flag. Of course, this had to be done on each end of the field, and in the middle if there was a middle ditch. It took work and care in placing the flags. The counting had to be perfect; otherwise, the wrong row would be changed.

Chores

By this time, I could use the milking machines and milk the cows. Leslie and I often worked together at this task. I did not like having to do chores early in the morning and again late in the afternoon, usually after working a long day in the fields. Otherwise, I did enjoy milking cows. Each cow had her own personality.

Three-spot was a very tall cow. She was cantankerous and could not be trusted. You best not walk close to her as you crossed behind her. She had a wicked kick, but worse, she could slap a fly from your nose with her tail; although, she preferred slapping your face, especially on very cold mornings. She was not especially good at producing milk. I am sure she was never an economical producer of milk. Her huge body took much grain to sustain.

Daisy was a short, docile cow. She always behaved, except sometimes when entering the barn, she would try to steel another cow's grain before going to her stall. She had a huge utter and was one of our better milk producers.

May was just a big, friendly dog. She would follow me around in the corral until I scratched her behind her horns and slapped her on her neck. If I were standing by her neck, she would move her head around until her head and neck encompassed me. She wanted me to scratch the other side of her neck. She would not always go directly to her stall. She would stand in the center of the barn, blocking the entrance of the other cows, and demand that I tickle her ears and behind her horns.

In the summer, Mom always had a huge garden. She needed fresh vegetables for each day's meal for the workers. Excess vegetables, and by design there were always excess vegetables, were canned and used during the fall and winter. We all shared garden duty. Often after a grueling day irrigating or in the field and after milking the cows, we got to hoe and irrigate the garden. By the time we were done, it was dark. We ate supper and went to bed.

Corn Shelling

Each year, all the sheds and bins filled with ear corn had to be emptied by calling a corn sheller. We had a corn-shelling day. It was a big day. This could happen anywhere from early spring to early fall. The cribs were emptied when the price was right, or to make way for the new corn crop. Many neighbors had trucks with which they would welcome the chance to earn extra money by hauling grain to town. The going rate was two cents per bushel.

Ralph Rose, the owner of the sheller, always arrived early. George helped him to set up his truck so that he could unload the shelled corn onto trucks and create a pile of cobbs. Each piece of equipment had to be in a special place. It had to be carefully planned so as not to create a problem later. Ralph was paid two and a half cents per bushel shelled.

Then the truckers arrived. They lined up in the order that they arrived. Then the shovelers arrived. That was George and the other hired men. Then Ralph revved up his engine and engaged the dragline that drug the ears of corn into the sheller. The noise was almost unbearable, especially when the corn entered the sheller to have the kernels of corn separated from the cobb.

One of my duties was to man the cobb wagon. When the cobb wagon filled, I pulled it out and placed another wagon in its place. I then took the cobbs into the corral and piled them in an area to allow for a nice place for the steers to sleep dry. Some of the cobbs were saved to shovel into the basement for burning. We also placed cottonwood logs there to burn. The cobbs were used to ignite the wood, since cobbs were easy to start on fire.

The dragline was under the floor of the crib and gravity took care of filling it for a few hours. Then we used a special fork to drag corn into the dragline. After a while, it was impossible to pull any more corn into the hopper with the special fork. This was when the shoveling started. It required anywhere from three to five men to keep the hopper filled. It depended on how far away the corn was.

The dinner had to be spectacular because there were many men, and they were hungry. Mom did not have to provide dinner for Ralph or the truck drivers. They were independent contractors. Mom always had meat and potatoes and corn, but on this day, she had a couple of different kinds of pie and maybe ice cream. It was important that the men return to work full. She did not want any of them gossiping that dinner at the Beck's was subpar. Mom was an excellent cook, and no one had the opportunity to complain about the food at her table.

Occasionally, the sheller would break down and Ralph had to turn off the engine. The silence was precious. We all sat and waited for Ralph and George to repair the broken chain, or whatever else had broken. Then the noise started again.

It was at this time, after the shoveling was removing more and more of the ears of corn, that all the kids, dogs, and cats formed a ring around the crib. It was when the rats realized they had to make a run for it. We could see a dog jump into action and chase down a rat, then a cat, then I might find one with a shovel. By the end of shelling, the yard was filled with dead rats. Only a few escaped. The interesting thing was that the next morning, all the dead rats had disappeared.

Church

Every Sunday, religiously, Mom made us boys put on our suits and the girls put on their best dresses and we attended Sunday school and then church services. I hated it. I would rather stay home. It was our only day off and I wanted to spend it doing fun things. We already had to milk the cows twice. That was enough punishment, but Mom was unyielding.

Dad never went to church. He got up on Sunday and went to the shop to piddle around fixing some tractor. Sometimes he got into his truck and visited the farms to see if anything needed immediate attention. Dad never stopped. He was always doing something, just not going to church.

Once Dad had a leveling job on which he was behind. The soil was wet, and the tractors often became stuck, which extended the time needed to finish the job. When one scraper became stuck, it stopped two scrapers because another one had to stop to pull the first scraper out. If they were not successful, then two scrapers were linked by chain to pull out the first. Dad liked to keep his word, so on one Sunday, Dad went to drive a scraper to advance the leveling. However, he immediately became stuck. He left that scraper and grabbed another one; however, that one also became stuck. On Monday morning, all the drivers arrived to find all but one tractor, stuck.

On another Sunday, Dad again was behind on a job. This time he did not become stuck. When he came home for dinner, after we were home from church, he asked Leslie and me if we wanted to earn money. Of course, we did. So, against Mom's protests, the three of us went to the field and advanced the work in that field. I loved it. We were paid in cash at the end of the day. How great was that! And Dad was happy! Mom, not so much.

Underground Fort

I had a phase when I liked to dig holes. Our soil was sandy, so it was easy to dig. I chose a spot between the chicken house, corn crib, and a couple of trees. No machinery could reach it, and no one even walked there; therefore, no one would bother my digging.

I dug down six feet. I was throwing dirt out of the hole above my head. Then I dug a second hole six feet away from the first one. My plan included a tunnel connecting the two holes. I dug the tunnel, making it just bigger than my body width. Finally, it was done! I tried it out. It worked perfectly. I never considered the possibility of the sandy tunnel collapsing—until Mom told me. She ordered me to stop digging. I could not. I somehow needed to dig a little each day.

One day I went to dig and thought the hole was not as deep as I had left it a couple of days before. I started digging and after digging six inches, a horrible smell hit me. I dug more and found that there were several packages of meat that had spoiled. Mom found a hole already dug and a way to discourage me from digging. Apparently, a small freezer had died, and much meat had spoiled. She needed a spot to dispose of it. That is when she thought of my already dug hole. That ended my hole-digging phase.

The New Machine Shed

Our current shop was now too small to hold all the tools and equipment needed to repair machinery. Dad had also bought several tractors, pull-combine, and other machinery. These should not be left outside to suffer from exposure to the weather. Dad decided we needed a much larger shop/machine shed.

One day in the fall, two local carpenters came and started making measurements. They measured an outline that was about eighty by one hundred and twenty feet. For me, it was huge. They poured the concrete foundation and a smaller floor area inside that would be the shop portion of the building. The remaining area would remain with a dirt floor.

Next, they made a form for making the girders that would hold the metal roof. These supported the steel shell in a steep arch starting at one end of the foundation and reaching the other side of the foundation. They were gigantic. They were more than thirty feet high in the center.

They started laying the one-by-fours around the prefabbed form by bending each board and nailing another board to it. When done, these giant girders were four boards thick, making the wooden girders at least four inches by four inches. As each girder was finished, a farm loader picked it up and manipulated it into place, where it was secured. Then another and another girder was finished. After they had three or four girders secured, they added the cross boards, which were one-by-threes laid about every two feet. The presence of these boards added stability to the vertical girders and gave more places to secure the steel shell.

When all girders were in place, the metal shell was added. I loved climbing up and over the structure before the metal shell was added. Then the day came when the building was complete, and it was time to move the tools into the new shop and the machinery into the machine part of the building. Dad was happy.

1957 (ten years old, fifth grade)

This was a year of changes. Life for me was moving faster and faster, and I liked it.

Bootsy Died

Bootsy meant a lot to all of us. During the winter of 1957, she grew weak and then weaker. After a lingering illness, she died. Dad took her to the vet for an autopsy. She died from diabetes. In those days, farmers did not take their pets to a vet, ever. It was the custom of the day.

Dad Bought a New Quarter (his second)

Early in the spring, Dad bought a 160-acre farm located next to George's quarter. He aggregated all the government set-aside acres and placed them on that farm. What was left was planted to oats. We started leveling the farm as soon as Dad had title. Leslie and I did the work. We worked into the summer. As soon as we had leveled the set aside land, the Dad and George harvested the oats, and we leveled that land. By fall, we had leveled the entire farm with wells drilled and pumps placed. The yields on the farm before we bought the farm were low. Our first year farming it, we more than doubled the yield.

Dad told me a story about when Leslie and I were leveling the quarter. We were working on the far side of the farm, one-half mile from the road. I had noticed that one car stopped on the road, and then two and then three. After a while they left. I thought no more of it. Dad said that they saw scrapers moving about with no visible driver. Leslie and I were not big enough for the on-lookers to see us driving the scrapers.

During this time, Leslie and I milked the ten or twelve cows as soon as we woke up. Then we had a quick breakfast and we off to scrape by 7:00 a.m. We drove the scrapers until 6:00 or 7:00 p.m. and hurried home to milk the cows. Sometimes, after a quick supper, we worked in the garden until dark.

A Wet Spring

The spring of 1957 was wet. It was difficult to plant on time because the soil never dried enough to permit it. Since our farm was part of the Platte River valley, it was sandy and had a high-water level. Sometimes we could see the water level because we could monitor it by looking at the water level in the road ditches. In lower lying land, the water level was above ground.

Dad was now growing more sorghum because it used less water and therefore, required less labor. This year the sprouting milo was yellow with weak stalks. Dad wondered if he would even have a crop in the fall. We had no tractor that could pull a go-dig (a cultivating device used before the more drastic cultivator itself) through the fields without getting stuck.

One day a truck arrived with an old, small Ford tractor with a small go-dig that hooked to the three-point-hitch. Dad hoped that this tractor armed with a go-dig could make it through the field when the other tractors could not. They evaluated it and it worked. Guess who they tasked with the job of go-digging a couple of hundred acres of sorghum? Yours truly.

The job required driving very slowly because I had to be careful not to cover the weak stalks of sorghum with dirt. It took forever to cross the field and forever to return. On a good day, I could only cover fewer than twenty acres. It was the most monotonous job I have ever had. I hated it. Worse, there were tad poles and young toads in the areas with water. I had to run them over and I did not like that. I had no choice because they were everywhere. If I tried to avoid them, I would not make it through the field even once.

The idea was that turning the soil would allow oxygen to penetrate for the root system to grow and it would allow the water to drain better. And so, it was. The sorghum became a little greener and the water dissipated quicker. Dad started to become more optimistic, especially when the sun shown more and began to dry the soil surface.

Tilling the Set Aside Acres

There was a government program that allowed farmers to not plant (set aside) a sizable portion of their tillable acres. For this, the government paid the farmer a set amount; however, the farmer had to maintain the land weed free. After go-digging, I used the JD 60 and a disk to till the set aside. I went back and forth on every field of set aside that we had. It was hot and dusty work. It was good to see the weeds chewed up by the disk, but a few always escaped. That bothered me, but I would get them the next time I tilled.

Land Leveling

During this summer, Leslie was mostly driving a scraper. He left with the men at 7:00 a.m. and did not return until nearly 7:00 p.m. He helped me with the morning chores because I also had to be ready to go with another hired man, but at night, I had the chores done before Leslie arrived from scraping.

During the fall, Dad decided it was time for me to learn how to drive a scraper. He gave me the Oliver 88 with the five-yard scraper and took me to a field. He pointed out the high point and the low point in the field. He told me to make them go away. At first, I was cutting too deep and dumping my dirt in an unsightly pile, but with time, I learned to finesse the blade and made shallower cuts and fills. I was still not particularly good, but that fall was only the start of my career as a scraper driver.

Dad had more business than he could hope to accomplish with the two scrapers. He bought a second eight-yard scraper and another JD 820 and then a third eight-yard scraper and yet another JD 820.

Dad was busy driving in all directions. He had clients as far away as forty miles. This taxed Dad's ability to flag, survey and map all new jobs and to check the scrapers' progress. Towards the end of each job, Dad had to survey for corrections and, sometimes, wait until they were done, especially if they were the final corrections. Sometimes the initial corrections left enough work to be done that Dad could leave the site and visit another site while the scrapers finished the corrections on the first site.

Dad was very adamant about quality. The final task was to float the field twice, once from one angle and then perpendicular to that angle. A sizeable rain without any water standing was the final test. After a good rain, Dad would jump in the pickup and drive to all the recent jobs to see if there was any water standing. If there was, and no crops had been planted, Dad volunteered to return to the site and correct it. He guaranteed his work.

Uncle Wayne was beginning to become involved in the survey work because Dad had a tough time being in so many different places at the critical times while managing the farm. Uncle Wayne was an excellent surveyor and could handle jobs located in the southern territory while Dad worked the remaining territory. Dad could not drive fast enough to cover everywhere.

Dad's workload was affecting his health. He suffered from ulcers and carried a supply of liquid medicine, which he drank like milk while he was driving seventy miles an hour down a country road. He maintained a significant inventory on his dashboard. He also suffered from migraines which would often force him to stop all activity. In those days, there were no viable medications; therefore, he had no choice but to remain immobilized until they passed. That made Uncle Wayne's participation even more important. He kept the business moving forward while Dad was at home sitting in his chair with his eyes closed and motionless.

I was kept busy floating all these jobs. I floated them twice and then had to go all around the perimeter twice. Every time I hit the end of the field, I had to raise the blade to make the turn. That deposited a pile of dirt that had to be spread out after I finished the second pass floating.

Once during the hottest part of the summer, I had a large field to float. It would take all day to finish. Dad came and picked me up for lunch, but on the return trip, I forgot my water jug. I told Dad, but there was nothing he could do because we had long since left home. I had to survive without water. Back and forth I drove and slowly crept across the field. I was already thirsty, and it was only approaching the hottest part of the day. My mouth was so dry. Finally, I finished once across the field. Then came the second pass. I did not think I could do it. In my favor was that I had the Oliver 99, which had enough power to pull the float faster than a smaller tractor would have been able to do.

After a few hours, I finished the second pass. Now, I should have made the two trips around the perimeter, but I was so very thirsty, that I could not do it. I needed water. It was late afternoon and I still needed to drive ten miles to be at home. I had to round a corner in order to pass through a small gate with the float. The float was thirty feet long and was not easy to maneuver. I swung out as far as the fence would permit and then brought the tractor through the gate, but the back of the float was catching the gate post. I backed up and tried again and again. I was dying of thirst. Finally, I drove the float over the man's gate post and headed home. I told Dad about the gate post. I forgot to tell him about not smoothing the perimeter of the field. He asked me about it. The client called and complained to Dad. I explained my being excruciatingly thirsty. Dad never reprimanded me. He understood.

Irrigation

Dad partnered me with a hired man who could drive the pickup. I knew what we had to do and when we had to do. The hired man drove me to the irrigation sets and helped with the work. We started at 7:00 a.m. and the hired man's day ended at 6:00 p.m. That is when I started the chores. I was done by 7:00 p.m. when Leslie arrived home.

Grandpa's land and Dad's land were now leveled such that center ditches were eliminated. All sets were longer because they now went from fence to fence. And we had aluminum tubes. In fact, we had tubes sized: ½, ¾, 1, 1 ¼, 1 ½, and 2 inches. Factors that we took into consideration before choosing the tube size included the length of the run, if it was the first time we irrigated the field, how far we were into the irrigation season, and weed growth. Dad carried a large inventory of each size of tubes.

The first week of irrigation was difficult. George got the JD 60 and ditcher out. The rest of us picked up our spades and followed. George had to make two passes to obtain a deep ditch. I usually road on the back of the ditcher to help it keep its blade in the ground. Then we had to dig out every other row because each row of water irrigated the row on each side of it. To dig out the rows, we had to remove the dirt from next to the side of the ditch. This was to allow the tube to be set deeper in the row. If we did not dig out the row, the end of the tube would be higher than the water level in the ditch and the tube would not start. The deeper we dug, the faster the water would flow. A set often would have from twenty to forty tubes; therefore, we needed to dig out that many rows to make that first set.

We started the irrigation well and we had to wait for it to fill the ditch. The first time took longer because the ditch was rough and dry. It had to melt the sand clods before it could proceed. We distributed the tubes and waited. It always took a larger sized tube to get the water to the end of the row the first time because it too had to melt the clods and form a smoother path down the row. This was where I started to get my hand callouses. By the time school started, my entire palm of my hand had a thick callous.

The second time we irrigated a field, we switched out the tubes and placed a smaller tube because the first set had formed the water channel. This time the water ran much quicker. We normally had to irrigate each field every five days. It was normal to irrigate each field fifteen to twenty times a season.

Part of the task of irrigation was to count rows to determine which rows had water that reached the end and which ones had not. This was not easy in a field that was one half mile by one quarter mile. Dad decided that we should count twenty rows and place a red flag (ten tubes). On the 100th row (50th tube) we would place a blue flag. On the 120th row, we would place a blue flag and a red flag. Upon reaching the 200th row (100th tube) we would place a white flag. This had to be done, without mistake, on both ends of the fields.

For each set, we knew in which row we had placed the first tube and we knew in which row the last tube was set. Using this, it was easy to count rows. Once we knew which rows were down, we pulled those tubes and distributed them among the rows that were not down. We usually had to do this a couple of times before one set was complete, and it was time to start a new set. We tried to have a new set each morning, afternoon, and evening.

Sometimes I convinced the hired man to allow me to drive the pickup while on the home place. I liked to drive fast and take corners without slowing down much. I would drive between the corn field and a shelter belt. Sometimes I would drive the truck into escaped irrigation water and get the truck stuck. The hired man walked on to make the irrigation set and I walked home to retrieve a tractor and chain.

My New Friends, Gordon and Tippy

After the school year ended, but before planting, we received a new neighbor. Mr. Wemhoff moved into a farmstead one mile from our place. With him, he brought a wife and twelve children. The oldest boy was my age, Gordon. I met Gordon after his dad finished planting his crop. He visited Dad to ask for a job and he brought Gordon. We immediately hit it off and from that moment on, we played together every Sunday after church

Mr. Wemhoff was the hardest worker I had ever seen. He could do his farm work before coming to work for Dad, and after he returned home at night. The scraper drivers usually quit at 6:00 p.m. and that left Mr. Wemhoff two or three hours of sunlight to work on his farm.

Gordon's family had a horse. I had never ridden a horse, so I begged Gordon to catch the horse so we could ride it. We rode bareback, everywhere. We went up the road and then down the road. We road around the pasture, but finally, the horse had to rest. Afterwards, I had a hard time walking. When I got home, I looked in the mirror to see what was hurting. I found two large blisters, one on each check. I did not walk or sit easily for a week. That curried me from horse riding.

One day Gordon told me that their dog had had puppies and they were already the size to adopt. I begged Mom and Dad, but they firmly said no. I walked over to Gordon's place one Sunday and saw the puppies. I saw one that I loved. They offered it to me for free. I grabbed it and walked home while holding it in my arms. Mom and Dad were not happy when they saw me. I told them not to worry because he was only "on trial." Tippy became a member of our family and was inseparable from Dad. He went everywhere with Dad.

The next summer when Dad was traveling from one group of scrapers to another, he was hungry. He stopped at the Dairy Queen in Central City and bought an ice cream cone for himself and another for Tippy. Tippy laid down and placed the cone between his paws and started licking the cone. As he licked, he kept turning the cone, so he ate evenly around the cone. Later, Dad discovered that Tippy liked chocolate cones better than vanilla. At that time, we did not know that chocolate was bad for dogs. Tippy did not seem to care.

Sometimes, when Dad was surveying, Tippy would become bored and start exploring the area. Unfortunately, when Dad was ready to leave, and he was always in a hurry, Tippy would be no where to be seen. Dad would cuss and fume while he searched for Tippy. After a while, he always managed to find him, except for a couple of times. One day he absolutely could not find Tippy, and he simply had to go to the next scraping site. If Dad were late, three or four scrapers would stop, and he could not allow that. He left before he found Tippy. Dad was crushed.

Dad would always swing around to the area where he lost Tippy and look for him. The next day, he saw Tippy trotting along the side of the road, heading home. Dad was never so glad to see him as Tippy was to see Dad.

The same thing happened a second time and Dad had to find Tippy, and he did not find him when he returned to look for him. Dad left for home absolutely crushed with worry. Dad fussed all night. During the night he could not sleep. He got up and returned to the work site and found Tippy exactly at the spot where he lost him.

New School in Town

The year before, during a local election, the town people passed a vote for the consolidation of their school district with our one-room-country school. This was done over the objections of the people living in the one-room-country school district. The city was enlarging their school by adding new rooms for kindergarten through third grade and an auditorium. The addition was not yet ready. Since the town school did not have room to accommodate us, they allowed us to attend one more year in the one-room-country school. That would have been my fourth-grade year. During that year we had town school bus service and subsidized milk for drinking.

Now, it was time to start my fifth grade in the big town school. I was nervous because I could not imagine how it would be inside such a large school. I was already used to riding the school bus, so that was not a problem, but on the first day of school, I became nervous. I did not want to dress or eat breakfast and I dreaded walking outside to the driveway to wait for the bus. The two-mile bus ride into town took forever. I did not want it to arrive, ever. The bus turned into a dead-end street and pulled up to the back end of the school. I did not want to leave the bus, but I did. I slowly followed the other kids through a double door into a hallway. Some kids went left to the new school, but all the big kids were taking a right and going up the steps. I wished I knew where I was going. As we reached the top of the stairs, teachers were there asking us our grade and then pointing to a room. By now, since we were late, all the classrooms were full of students. Each classroom had as many students as we had in our entire one-room school. There were three of us joining the class and there were three empty seats scattered about. I was so nervous as I headed toward an empty seat. I felt that everyone was looking at me. They were.

During the first recess, I discovered they had an indoor toilet. Everyone went outside to play. I just followed the other kids, but I only watched the others. I was too nervous and shy to join. Soon, I became acquainted with the other kids and joined them in their games. It was not so bad. Just a lot more people.

End of Irrigating Season

At the end of each irrigation season, the hundreds of different sized tubes had to be stored for the next year's irrigation. That was my job. We went to each irrigation well and gathered the tubes by throwing them into the pickup. We took them to an area by a truck shed and piled them. They were an entangled mess. As the pile grew higher and wider, my job started.

I sorted the tubes by diameter and length and then gathered them into groups. Each size tube had a different number of tubes in a batch. I might gather fifteen two-inch tubes or fifty one-half-inch tubes. The idea was to make a group of a manageable and consistent size. Once I had the necessary number of tubes, I had a metal band that I wrapped around each end of the tubes. I then crimped a clamp on each one and cut the band. At the end of each day, I carried the tubes to the shed where I had to store them in the shed's attic. To move the tubes up to the attic, there was a hoist. I hoisted each bundle up to the next floor, then I climbed up and recovered the bundle. I tried to place each bundle with others of the same size so they would be sorted by size. It took forever, but I enjoyed it.

The fall weather had its crisp, but sunny, breeze. I loved being outside with a long-sleeved shirt and feeling comfortable as I worked. I liked watching the men working on the combine and otherwise preparing for the harvest. The rustle of the cottonwood grove behind and the smell of drying vegetation was appreciated.

Putting Up Silage

Every year Dad cut silage for the cattle that he would buy later in the fall. This year he was planning on buying more cattle than he usually did, so, we had to cut more silage than usual. Dad rented a couple of acres on the neighbor's building site where we could make the pile. It was catawampus from where we would be cutting the sileage. This made the hauling of each load of silage easier.

The cutting started after we started school. I wanted to be present to see it all happen. There was so much activity. Dad and George drove the silage cutter. A couple of other men drove the wagons. When one wagon was filled, it was unhooked from the silage cutter and another empty wagon was connected. Everything had to be fast and efficient. Dad was an impatient man. Once the silage arrived at the pile, if the wagon had a hydraulic hoist, it was pulled up the pile and dumped. The driver then lowered the hoist and scurried back to collect another load.

Dad had many wagons without hydraulic hoists, so Dad and George devised a plan to quickly dump their loads. They laid out a chicken wire mesh in the bottom of the wagon and up the front. At that end they bolted a board on each side with a place to attach a log chain. The wagon was pulled up the pile and stopped. Another tractor driver backed up to the wagon while another man attached a log chain to the chicken wire. The driver slowly drove away pealing the chicken wire back neatly, emptying the wagon in just seconds.

This tractor then returned to its other job of packing the silage to drive out the oxygen. The more oxygen left in the pile, the more spoilage that occurred during the winter. The tractor had to be heavy to better pack the silage.

Another man had a tractor with a blade. Besides smoothing each wagon's clump of silage, he also helped compacting the silage. Each day the silage pile grew taller, making it more dangerous for the tractor drivers. The higher the pile, the easier for them to tip over backwards. They all now backed up the pile. I was not allowed to drive any of the tractors for this reason. The goal was to make the pile as tall as possible while minimizing the base because the thin layer was lost to spoilage. Often the top six inches to one foot was lost to spoilage; therefore, we wanted a minimum base. This resulted in a tall, and more dangerous, silage pile.

Mom Slaughters Broiler Hens

Every year Mom raised a couple of hundred broiler hens from chicks. We cleaned the brooder house to prepare for their arrival. When they arrived, we kept them in small boxes, each with a pair of brooder heat lamps hanging over them to keep them warm.

Slowly, they grew and at the end of the summer, or early fall, they were ready for processing. Mom went into the pen and brought out three or four chickens by their feet. She placed one on the ground and then placed a short board over its neck. She pulled hard separating the head from the body. Then she threw the body to the ground where it flopped around for a while as she prepared the next chicken and the next.

She had a tub of boiling water over a small fire. She placed each chicken into the water for a little bit and then she plucked the chicken of all its feathers. She washed the chicken and finalized the plucking before she placed it into a plastic bag and placed it in an empty freezer. Before she finished, the freezer was full. It was with these chickens and a head or two of beef that we fed the family and our hired men.

Dad Builds a Swimming Pool

Dad recognized that we worked hard and wanted to give us more chance to recreate. He decided to dig a swimming pool in our back yard. He took the JD 60 with its loader and started to dig a hole. When he finished, he had a hole that was twenty feet wide and sixty feet long. It was six inches deep at the shallow end and eight feet deep at the deep end. Every day, when we returned from our school day, we checked on the progress of the pool. After digging the hole, they placed a wire mesh along the sides and bottom. They mixed concrete and spread it around only about three to four inches thick. Once the concrete dried, they painted it.

Dad had already placed a four-inch well beside it. With the well, he filled the pool. To our chagrin, it was far too cold to swim in because it was fall. He left the water in the pool during the winter to equalize the pressure on the sides so that the thin concrete sides would not collapse. We ice skated on the ice during the winter.

The next summer, it was a community event to empty the water and then refill the pool. The kids from town and other people were welcome at the pool. On summer days there was a line of kids walking two miles from town to our pool. Dad had cleaned an area in the garage and made it into a place where people could change clothes if they wanted.

Dad's lawyer worried about the liability that was created by having a pool. He convinced Dad to build a four-foot fence around it to keep people out of the pool when we were not home.

Occasionally, Leslie and I used the pool on Sundays and evenings. We were often too tired to use it and, after eating supper, we migrated to our beds to rest for the next day's activities.

Hunting Pheasants and Quail with Grandpa Tyler

After harvest when the hunting season opened, Leslie and I loved it when Grandpa Tyler and all the uncles would come to our farm to hunt for pheasants and quail. They brought their hunting vests filled with shot and Uncle Paul brought his hunting dogs. We went to each fence line and walked it. Leslie and I were kept on the outside of the hunting line for safety reasons. We had to prove our safety precautions before we had a chance at a better spot in the line.

I loved watching the dog's work. They stopped and pointed and then, when we were ready, they flushed the birds. Grandpa and my uncles were excellent hunters. They had been hunting since they were ten years old. I do not remember if Leslie killed any birds, but I never did. I hunted with a single-shot 410 gauge. For safety reasons, due to my inexperience, I had to walk with the gun open; however, I could leave the shot in the barrel. It gave me a chance to become accustomed to the hunt without endangering any of the other hunters.

Hunting Ducks and Geese with Grandpa Tyler

Leslie and I were excited. Grandpa Tyler had invited us to hunt with him and the uncles. They had built a hunting blind on a tiny island in the Platte River where they often hunted during the hunting season. It was cold and there was ice in the river. Since we were leaving early in the morning, Dad took us over to stay the night before. Spending the night with Grandma and Grandpa was reason to be excited but going hunting with the family—we were ecstatic.

Grandpa and all the uncles had their hip-wader boots with all the necessary equipment for such a hunt. Leslie and I only had our regular rubber boots that we did chores in. They only went to below our knees. For wading in the Platte River, I was fearful that the cold water would overrun my boots, because halfway to my knees still was not very high.

Somehow Grandma fed us and got us to bed at a reasonable time. We had to arise early the next morning, far earlier than we were accustomed to rising. Sure enough, no more than we had slept, and Grandma was calling us that the coffee was ready. She had been up for awhile already fixing breakfast. Grandpa and Joe were up checking their equipment. We were told to get dressed quickly, check our equipment, and eat breakfast, which we did. We could not hold Grandpa back. He would simply leave us. Hunting was a passion, and no grandson would spoil a good day of hard-earned hunting. The rest of the uncles arrived, and we were off. It was so very cold that morning; I thought I was going to die.

We arrived at the riverside before the truck had a chance to warm us. We got out and collected our things. Grandpa and the uncles had sandwiches and hot coffee with them. They reached the river's edge and slowly felt for the river's bottom before taking their first step. Each step they took was measured, always evaluating the water because the river's bottom was known to be uneven. Leslie entered the water. Finally, it was my turn. I was scared that the water would overflow my poor boots. Relieved, the water only reached halfway up my boots. I slowly took each step. The water was swifter than it was during the summer because upstream they were releasing more water from a dam.

Halfway to the hunting blind, the water was increasingly deeper. At one point, it came within one inch of the top of my boot. I was terrified, especially since it was still dark. I only had the moon to tell me how afraid I should be. Finally, we reached the blind. We all entered and sat down. Grandpa and the uncles had a cup of coffee. Leslie and I did not yet drink coffee. It was so cold. Now, we just waited for the sun to rise. Earlier, the uncles had positioned the duck and geese decoys. Now, all we had to do was wait.

We were inside a closed blind, so we could not see the sunrise other than the little light that came through the door. When it did brighten the inside of the blind, I saw a sheet of paper with a cartoon on it hanging from the wall. It asked the question why Texans do not wear Bermuda shorts. Under it was a huge drawing of a smiling Texan, with a huge cowboy hat with his two testicles hanging out from under his Bermuda shorts. I died laughing. They quickly told me to shut up. I did.

Once, I stuck my head out the door and saw Grandpa's duck and geese decoys. He made them himself out of cottonwood chunks that he carved with and a hatchet. He had one long stick in the bottom which he thrust into the bottom of the river to secure them. He had another stick which he used for a neck and finally, a head carved from a small wooden block. Some might have been painted at some point in time. They served their purpose, plenty of ducks and geese landed in their midst expecting a party.

Eventually ducks and geese came, and one uncle started using his duck or goose call. We watched as the ducks or geese considered the call. Some even started a descent, but at the last moment, they were off again.

Grandpa and my uncles were growing restless. Finally, a group of ducks came in for a landing. Grandpa and my uncles dropped the side window and started firing. It was all over before I was in position. They had managed to drop several ducks. The hunting dog was gone in a flash and brought back the ducks.

The same thing happened with geese. After several hours, they had reached their limit and we started the reverse process to the trucks, only this time the uncles had several birds attached to their belts. The birds would immediately be dressed and refrigerated. The geese would have their down and soft feathers saved for use in pillows and blankets for the bed. Every useful part of the geese was saved and utilized.

I was so glad to be back at Grandma's where Leslie and I had hot chocolate. We told every detail to her, but she did not seem as excited as we were. Finally, Dad came, and we went home. They gave us a goose to have on Sunday instead of chicken.

End-of-Year Special Employee Dinner

Dad started a custom of celebrating the end-of-harvest and the end-of-scraping, by inviting all hired men and scraper drivers to Dorothy Lynch's restaurant in St. Paul, Nebraska for dinner. Dad rented the entire restaurant. This was before she commercialized her salad dressing. Every employee was asked to bring his wife and all their children. They could order anything on the menu with an open bar. When Dad threw a party, he threw a party.

I have been told that the men really looked forward to that event. It was meant to be a time of happiness where Dad showed his appreciation toward the men that allowed him to be in business. Dad genuinely appreciated them.

Unfortunately, Dad was in a good mood and started drinking Canadian Club whiskey sours. With each one, he became happier. I do not think he ate anything too because he was constantly walking around visiting with his men. He wanted to make sure their families would order anything their heart pleased. He also tipped handsomely everyone from dishwasher to cook to server. I do not know how many drinks Dad had consumed, but on the way home, Mom drove in fuming silence. She did not like alcohol in the house or Dad consuming it. Although Dad, too, was silent, he had a smile on his face. His men had genuinely enjoyed themselves. Dad had too.

Playing in the Haymow

When I was bored in the winter, I put on warm clothes and went to the haymow. There was only one weak light placed on the ceiling which was twenty feet high and covered with decades of dust. I surveyed the inventory of straw and hay bales. Some were located almost twenty feet high; they were leftovers from when the barn was full of bales. I made forts. They had high positions protected by bales stacked two-high as a guard rail. Behind them was a tunnel connecting that spot with another higher position. And there was always the highest position for lookout. It had to be positioned so that it could be protected from the side with more bales. It was a work of art. Then Leslie, or Dad, or George would come and throw down straw bales to accommodate the pigs or alfalfa bales to keep the cows fully nourished during the winter and destroy my fort's structure. I was always disappointed.

Packing Grease in Ball Bearings

One Saturday during the winter when the temperature was in the low 20's, Dad decided it was the perfect day to load grease into bearings. Earlier in the year, Dad had brought spare parts back from Lubbock, Texas. Some of those parts included ball bearings for the scrapers. At that time, they came dry. They had no grease in them.

We went to our old machine shop to work. We had already closed the big doors, but there were gaps everywhere. The temperature inside was the same as it was outside. Dad had this fuel powered portable furnace that we started, and it blasted hot air into the shed. You could not feel the heat more than a few feet from the hot surface.

Dad brought out a five-gallon can of cold grease from somewhere and sat it a safe distance from the furnace. The idea was to soften the grease so we could dip it out of the can. George brought all the bearings that needed packing, and there were many of them. To start, we had to remove the gloves from both of our hands and dip one of them into the cold grease to get a handful. With the other hand, we grabbed the bearing and rubbed it against the grease to force the cold grease inside the bearing.

With time, the grease softened a little and the temperature climbed a little, but we worked all day, and it was still cold. I thought my hands would never again be warm.

1958 (11 years old, 6th grade)

Dad Bought Another Quarter (3rd Quarter)

During the winter, Dad bought another quarter section of land. This quarter was next to the other quarter and George's place and to the farm worked by Mr. Wemhoff. It was not outrageously rough, but it would need one-to-two-foot cuts and fills before irrigation would be possible. As usual, Dad placed all the government set aside acres on this farm so that we had the entire summer to level it at our leisure.

That year the new JD 730 came out with fifty-three horsepower. Dad bought one to replace the JD 60. The JD 60 would be retired from row crop work and used mostly to grind corn for the cattle. The JD 730 would better manage the disk, planter, and many other things that the JD 60 struggled with.

The Spring Harrow

Dad bought a new five-section harrow. It was too wide to travel on the roads without being folded. It was used in the last field operation before planting. Chemicals were not yet used in agriculture.

After finishing harrowing a field, I had to prepare the harrow for road travel. To do this, I had to take each section from the horizontal position and lift it to the vertical position. I was in good shape, but each section was still heavy. To accomplish this, I grabbed onto the last line of six-inch-long springs and slowly and carefully, lifted it above my head. Once there, I needed to secure it with a bolt; therefore, I needed to hold it with my left hand while using my right hand to place a bolt on a chain into a hole. The problem was that each section had fifty, or more, six-inch springs that were about $1/8^{th}$ of an inch wide with a very sharp end, sharpened by the point being drug many miles over the sandy soil. The problem was if I lost my grip on the harrow or stumbled and fell. Ten or more springs would have impaled me. I was incredibly careful and never fell.

First Color Television Set

Grandma and Grandpa Beck had recently purchased a colored television set. I was constantly begging Mom and Dad to visit them to watch TV shows in color, especially Bonanza on Sunday nights. Shortly afterward, when we came home from school our black and white TV was gone and a large colored TV was sitting in its place. It also had a record player built in. I did not care about the record player; I wanted the colored TV.

Sherilyn Swims in Deep End of Pool

In the summer, Sheri was in the pool every day. Sheri took swimming lessons with Barbara Morgan and became a good swimmer. She was like a little fish. After begging, Mom allowed her to swim across the deep end of the pool. She was the last one in the family to do this. Shannon and Shelli were already proficient swimmers and even dived from the diving board.

Wheat Harvest

That summer was hot. The wheat matured quickly. Dad had bought a new seven-and-a-half-foot pull combine. Dad pulled it with the JD 730. It was the largest combine in the area. Most people only had five-foot combines. Neighbors saw the new combine and asked Dad to custom combine their wheat. Dad did not turn down any opportunity to add to his cash flow, especially when he had a new combine to pay for.

Dad's deal was that I would accompany him to pull wagons with the JD 60 so Dad could empty the combine's grain bin while on the go. Dad was always in a hurry. He did not want to stop the combine long enough to empty the bin. It was hot and dusty, and a bad storm was expected that night. We had to finish this man's field and then we still had one unharvested field of our own to finish—no matter what. Everything had to be done before the storm came. We could see a dark cloud bank growing in the northwestern horizon.

Our problem was that parts of the field were wet. It was difficult for us to get our tractors through these locations. The problem was more so for me because I had to pull an ever-fuller wagon that was harder and harder to pull. Once Dad was unloading and we started to go through one of these soft spots when my tractor's tires started to spin in the mud. I was losing my ability to keep pace with Dad. Dad was watching somewhere else and did not notice me fading away. I yelled, but that did not help because of the extreme noise. Then he was emptying wheat onto the ground and then onto my head. Finally, Dad saw me slipping away and stopped. Finally, I got through the mud hole and caught him.

Again, we had forgotten the water jug and we were very thirsty, but Dad's only thought was to finish this field and then to finish our own field. By the time we finished this field, I was dying of thirst. I was certain that I would not make it. Then, we finished and started off to harvest our wheat located five miles away. This part went faster because there were no wet parts. The clouds were building and by now they were threatening us with rain, hail and whatever else was in green thunderheads filled with lightning and thunder.

Finally, Mom brought George to drive the truck filled with wheat home. We were a caravan: Dad with his new pull combine, me with a couple of wagons and George following us with the truck. As soon as we got home and were able to park our equipment inside the machine shed, the most terrible storm hit the area. Much of other farmers' unharvested wheat was lost.

Uncle Wayne Cuts Our Hair

At one point, each month we went to Uncle Wayne's house to have our hair cut. It helped to save money, but it was more for Dad and Uncle Wayne to socialize and plan hog production, farming and land leveling. They always had interesting discussions. I always wanted to be first because after my haircut, I could play with Dan and Brian.

Land Leveling

By this time Dad had a fleet of ten scrapers. Keeping them on several locations was difficult. It kept both Uncle Wayne and Dad busy. They had the initial flagging and surveying to be done, then the staking. Once the scrapers were working, their progress need to be checked periodically, especially when it was time to finalize each working lane. Typically, there would be the initial surveying for corrections, then after that work, there had to be a final check to ensure that everything was perfect. Only then could the machines leave the field. That is why it was so important that Dad or Uncle Wayne be there at the end of work for each field—to keep the machines from sitting there waiting for their approval to move to the next job.

Dad knew of Mr. Wemhoff's struggle with so many children and assigned him to level the new quarter. Mr. Wemhoff started at 6:00 a.m. and drove until 8:00 p.m. day after day after day, six days a week. He accumulated twelve to thirteen machine hours daily. These were the hours that paid the most, as opposed to the hours of stuck time, machine maintenance and fueling, which paid less. Mr. Wemhoff, by working so many hours, finished the quarter in no time. Mr. Wemhoff was a nice person. I always liked working with him. Gordon was old enough that he did the farming for the family.

One gloomy fall Saturday, Leslie and I were tasked with a scraper on a project near Central City. It was cold and neither of our JD 820's had comforters, so we were exposed to whatever the weather threw at us. We bundled ourselves as well as we could, but it was still cold. Back and forth we went. It rained occasionally, just enough to make us wet and make us miserable, and back and forth we went, smoothing each lane as best we could. Then we were in a blinding blizzard. At first, there was no accumulation, but eventually, it started to accumulate. Back and forth we went, dreaming of lunch time when we could sit in the pickup and warm up and dry off. It was hard to leave the pickup and start the afternoon, but we had no choice. Back and forth we went, with us carrying the wet dirt from a high spot to a low spot.

Eventually, it was nearly dark when we had to quit, go home, and milk the cows. After we finished the chores, we each took long hot shower. It was so wonderful. Then we ate supper and positioned ourselves in front of the fireplace. We appreciated the warmth emanating from the fireplace.

George Fell from Pickup

Dad was usually very stressed from having so many things to do that were so separated by miles and time. He was never patient and was always in a hurry. Once he and George were putting in cut and fill stakes for the scraper drivers to read. Dad was reading his large map in his lap, driving, and using a crayon to mark the stake. To save time, George held the door open and was only half-sitting in the sit so that he could jump out quicker to drive in the next stake. Dad saw that he had misread the map a few stakes back. Upon seeing this, he swore, accelerated rapidly while turning to the left. The result was that George tumbled out of the pickup and turned a somersault before coming to a rolling stop. At first, Dad did not notice George's absence. Only when he felt the pickup door swinging uncontrolled did he look and see George missing. That slowed Dad a bit and he turned back to see if George was unhurt. He was.

Late Corn Hilling

Late in the irrigation season, crabgrass had filled the area between the corn rows, making it difficult to get the rows' water to the end of their run. Corn yields were suffering. Dad bought a pair of stilts for the little Ford tractor. In the machine shop, he and George worked to set the tractor on the stilts. I have no idea how they managed it, but they did. Once done, the bottom of the tractor was seven or eight feet above the ground.

We had to remove all the siphon tubes from the ditches, allow the ditches to dry, and close the ditch before he could start re-hilling the corn. This cut the crabgrass between the rows of corn, casting it aside into the corn stalks. The row, thusly clear of weeds, would allow the water to flow again. But Dad had a problem. The hillers were not digging into the dirt enough. He asked Leslie and me to stand on the hiller blades. We did and Dad zipped through the field at high speed because there was no danger of the flying dirt covering the corn. The corn was already seven or eight feet tall. We spent days riding the hillers. It was not the most enjoyable work that I have done. I received leaf cuts from the sharp passing corn leaves.

After finishing each field, we had to open the ditch again and dig out the rows again. It was just like we did during the first week of irrigation, but we got the water to the end of the rows, so Mission Accomplished!

Harvesting and Selling Watermelons

Grandpa had always had a watermelon patch since he was a kid. He learned to save seed from the sweetest melons and plant then the following year. People came from several towns away to buy his melons. People had been coming for decades. They usually came on Saturdays, but especially on Sundays after church.

Usually on Fridays, he drove his pickup into the patch with kids, either Kathy, Dan and Brian from Uncle Wayne's family, or Leslie, me, Shannon, and Shelli from our family. Joe would drive the pickup. Grandpa would walk around the pickup and point at the melons that were ripe, and we would cut them from the vine and carry them to the pickup. Some were too large for one of us to carry, so we doubled up to transport them to the pickup.

When the pickup was full, we sat on the melons while Grandpa drove the pickup to his yard. He parked next to the old horse-drawn wagon. We transferred the melons to the wagon, which was parked next to the ancient and rusty balance used to weigh the melons. Then we went out to collect another pickup load. If we kids, including Joe, were helping him sell melons on Sunday and his inventory began to shrink, a couple of us would oversee the sales while Grandpa and the others returned for more melons.

Digging Grandpa's Potatoes

Every year in late August, but before school started, Grandpa would dig his five to ten acres of potatoes, which had been carefully cared for and irrigated. The week before the dig, Grandpa placed an ad in the local paper informing that the community was invited to pick up any potatoes that remained on Saturday, or after, for their own use.

On Friday, Grandpa had his old and small Allis-Chambers tractor hooked up to an even older potato digger. It dug one row at a time, threw the potatoes onto a tract that elevated them while shaking them. This was to eliminate any clods of soil that might be mixed in with the potatoes. Behind him, he left a wide string of freshly dug potatoes on the sandy soil surface.

Uncles Wayne and Paul had their pickups there along with their families. We had our pickup and Grandpa had his pickup. We each picked a row and started collecting potatoes down the row. We preferred the larger potatoes. I think some weighed two pounds. They were enormous. If the bucket were small, sometimes only one or two potatoes would fill them. We left at least half of the potatoes in the field. When our pickups were weighted down with potatoes, we filled Grandpa's pickup.

We formed a caravan and drove to Grandpa's place where we children carried his potatoes downstairs and placed them in their potato bin. We all had more than enough potatoes until the next year.

For days after we collected our potatoes, a dozen cars could be seen at the edge of the potato patch with city people filling gunny sacks and placing them in the back of their cars. Lower income families grew to depend on this opportunity to save money on their food budget. The community deeply loved my grandpa. He always gave back to it. He was a kind man.

Replacing Bicycle Flat Tires

My main mode of transportation was riding my bicycle. I rode it miles every day. The farmstead was large. I rode the bicycle from the house to the machine shed or to hay the cattle. We also suffered from a burr that we called Mexican sandbur. They were a seed with sharply pointed spears heading from the center outward in a random manner. The problem was that some of them were longer than ¼ inch and could penetrate a bicycle tire, and they often did.

When a tire suffered from a puncture, I first tried to repair the puncture. I removed the tire from the frame and then used a large screwdriver to pull out one side of the tire. That done, I removed inner tube and put a little air into it to find the leak. Then I used the grinder to rough up the area around the puncture. I placed the cement on the tire and then held the patch on the tube for a while. I waited until the next day to replace the tire.

Sometimes the tube was so damaged that I needed a new one. When this happened, I found the Sears and Roebuck catalog and looked for inner tubes. I had to write a letter ordering what I wanted and enclose a check with the proper tax included. I posted it the next day from our rural mailbox.

After a week, I became impatient and started looking for the mailman to come by every day. I went to the mailbox and was disappointed when it did not come. Sometimes it took two weeks to come.

The Lost Milk Cows

It was cold and snowing heavily with huge flakes floating to the ground, occasionally to be jostled about by wind gusts. Before going to bed, I pressed my nose close to the window to eliminate the reflection from the kitchen lights, and looked out the window. My nose told me it was cold. When the wind blew, I could only see a few feet, but when the wind was quiet; I could still only see a few yards. I could not see the barn that was tall, red, and close enough that my little sister could hit it with a baseball when she was playing by the garage. Tomorrow morning would not be pleasant. I already dreaded waking in the morning.

I went quickly downstairs and peeled my clothes layer by layer and carefully laid them by my bed to make them easy to replace in the morning. As I pulled the covers over my head, I heard Dad adding corn cobs to the furnace and then I heard each cottonwood log he threw into the belly of the furnace. He always placed the larger logs at night because they burned longer. It would be eight hours before the furnace would again be fed more logs. By early morning, there would only be warm coals in the furnace. Within two hours the house would start to cool and by morning, the house would be very cold; and the basement was the coldest place in the house. I hated stepping onto the cold cement floor at night.

The morning always came before it was invited. My alarm clock was Dad stoking the fire. He threw corn cobs in to help start the fire, and then filled the remaining area with cottonwood chunks, mostly midsized for its quick heat. As the fire started to warm, the furnace cracked and growled as if it also did not like being awakened so early either. Before he closed the furnace door, I had to be up and dressing. If not, he would call me, and that was not a good way to start the day.

I put on the clothes I left by my bed, which included two pair of thick socks. Then I went to the huge closet by the front door and added several layers of coats, including two or three gloves. Gloves were always too large for my small hands, and some had holes in the fingers. Usually, the combination of three gloves would keep out the cold.

The worst part of morning was opening the front door and receiving the first blast of freezing air. The complete darkness made it even colder. The snow was still falling heavily, and the wind was continuous. The drifting made it difficult to know, but I thought about ten or twelve inches of new snow had fallen during the night.

Struggling against the power of the wind, I opened the barn door, squeezed inside, and stepped back allowing the wind to close it. I turned on the lights, but they only added a small amount of light, like a flashlight with weak batteries, since they had many layers of fly specks on them. At least fifteen cats were hunkered together for warmth in a corner. The ones on the edge became cold and jumped into the center of the living mass; forcing others to move out and exposing a new group of cats to the cold outside edge. After a few minutes, the process was repeated.

I grabbed the feeding bucket and opened the wood door into the grain bin and filled it. The bucket was banged and bent in all places; yet, it had not changed a bit in ten years. It had to be fifty or a hundred years old. I went to each stall and placed the correct amount of each feed for those cows that were currently fresh. I returned the bucket to the feed bin and closed the door and fastened it so the cats could not enter and use it as a litter box. When it was cold, the cats used the feed bin as their personal litter box. It was much more convenient than going outside into the cold.

It was now time to bring the cows inside. I opened the back barn door, but there were no cows waiting to enter. I opened the door wider, but still no cows. I went into the cow yard and closed the door behind me, but I could see no cows. There was snow on the ground, and it was snowing hard. Visibility was poor. The cows were mostly white with a few black spots here and there. I could only hope to find the cows by finding the black spots. If they were standing in a group, it would be easier. If they were lying down or scattered; it would be hard to find them. I may not find them until it becomes light outside, but that would mean I would be late for school. School started at 8:30 o'clock and I had to be done milking by 7:30, if I were to have any hope of arriving on time to school.

The corrals were as large as a football field and contained a pole shed for shelter, a water tank, and a huge middle area for haying the cattle. I had to walk around every edge looking for the cattle. Nothing but white was visible. I explored each nook and crevice, and I found no cows. I did find the gate to the corn stalks, and it had been left open. It should have been closed. This opened an area one half mile by one half mile to the cows. This included two miles of fence line with trees, weeds, and brush. Outside the corral, the cows had many favorable places to spend the night, and they were all distant.

I muttered a few words that are not relevant and started up the lane towards the corn stalks. As I walked, I squinted to increase my chances of finding the cows, I kept my chin down to keep my neck warmer and I clapped my hands together to improve my circulation. I still could only see fifty feet as the morning was slowly becoming brighter. I walked and I walked, but no cows. Eventually, I found them. Most were huddled together for warmth, but a couple cows were happily eating fallen ears of corn. I rounded them up and tried to hurry them towards the barn. Early on that cold morning, the cows where not in a hurry, even though I tried to push them as much as I could.

Once I had them in the barn, I had to clean the cows utters with a warm rag. This required understanding of cow behavior; they did not favor having their udders touched with anything moist. Even a warm rag cools very quickly in weather this cold. I had to talk to them and pat them, so they were not focusing on any one spot. Sometimes it worked and sometimes they protested by slapping me in the face with their tails. They had exceptionally good aim and knew exactly the location of their target. Their tails, like their udders, were not very clean. Being struck in the face was unpleasant on many levels. It stunk and it stung as my skin was cold and more sensitive to being whipped.

Once the cow was prepared, I grabbed a bucket and a one-legged stool and scooted up close to her utter. I leaned my head onto her side, and that can also be very unpleasant as their sides were as clean as the cows' utters and tails, and we could not bath them, so we tolerated it. If I was lucky, they did not kick as their tits may have been sensitive or sore from the freezing weather.

The first cow's milk was used to fill the cats' pan. It had to be cleaned before I poured any milk. Cleaning consisted of taking the pan outside and knocking out any ice that was left. There were two pans to accommodate the fifteen cats that came leaping from everywhere. Some disagreements occurred since not all cats could eat at once, even with two pans. The ones with the highest social order and sharpest claws ate first. The pans emptied fast and usually more milk from the last cow was given to the cats. Cats were a very important part of mice and rat control on a farm and a little milk each day was not begrudged them.

If a cow had just freshened, her milk could not be saved for a few days, but she must be milked anyway, and her calf must be fed. I put about four inches of milk into the bottom of a bucket and enter the calf's pen where I must try to teach the calf to drink from a bucket. Nature had taught the calf to turn its head up to suckle from the cow. When the milk flow slows, the calf uses his head to butt the utter. The cow succumbs to this black mail and allows more milk to flow. This makes it difficult to teach a calf to drink. One can never be in a hurry. I liked this chore the least of all for my hands had to be bare to do this job and they were cold. When the calf butted the bucket, and it did about every five seconds, the milk flew everywhere, including on my clothes and face. My exposed fingers were freezing cold.

Everyone had his own favorite method of teaching a calf to drink. Some people became impatient and shouted verbal orders for the calf to drink. When it did not obey, the calves were punished. Of course, no learning was occurring. I placed my hand under the calf's chin and placed my fingers inside its mouth; then I tried to convince the calf to lower his head into the bucket. This is contrary to what nature has taught him. He would bite my fingers and butt the bucket, but sometimes he drank a small amount of milk. It required great patience and within about ten days, somehow, the calf would learn, and my life became more pleasant.

I placed the milk into the cream separator and separated the cream from the milk. We sold the cream, not the milk. The government requirements, even then, required much more cleanliness than could be obtained on a farm like ours. The cream was taken to the house and poured into a cream can. The cream truck passed once a week. The cream-less milk was given to the pigs. It was cold outside, and the milk was still warm. I carried it outside to their trough and poured it in. The trough was ten feet long and the pigs knew when I left the barn, so they were there waiting for me, already fighting and squealing; pushing and shoving. The stronger hogs secured positions near the head of the trough. The less strong were grateful for positions farther from the head, and the weaker hogs had no position at the trough. The buckets of milk never contained enough milk for the milk to reach the bottom end of the trough. There was never enough to satisfy them; a pig's position at the trough was important in determining how fast the hog fattened.

I had to clean the machines and release the cows. Then, I had to clean, change clothes, and eat breakfast. I arrived at school about forty minutes late that morning. Most students did not have two hours of chores to do before going to school every morning. I was self-conscious about arriving late for school, but there was nothing I could do.

Cutting Wood for Furnace

Periodically, the wood for the furnace in the basement had to be replaced. The process normally involved Dad locating a dead Cottonwood tree and driving his pickup there with a chainsaw. Leslie and I rode with Dad. George brought the large wagon with sideboards for us to load with wood.

Usually, the day had normal fall temperatures, and we even sweat while working. It was difficult work for Leslie and me because every log, small or large, had to be thrown over the wagon's sideboard, which was very high.

Growing Up on a Nebraska Farm

On this specific Saturday, the day was bitter cold with one to two feet of snow on the ground. We had to add layers of clothing to have a chance of not being cold. It was impossible to be warm. George first had to start the JD 60, because it had the loader with which George would dig out the snow for more than one-half mile to allow us to get to the nearest fallen Cottonwood tree. Next, George had to start the JD 730 to pull the wagon of wood. Starting a diesel engine in weather that cold was a challenging task, but one that George was up to. The tractors were left to warm up before we did anything with them.

When the JD 730 was warm, we hooked it up to the wagon. It had a comforter on it, but without a windscreen. That at least helped to channel the engine's heat back to warm the lower part of the body. The face and upper body were still exposed to the wind and cold. The JD 60 had no comforter on it, so George was exposed to the full force of the wind and cold.

George led the way out our driveway, down the road, and into the half-mile road to the fallen tree. He pushed the snow with the JD 60 and loader until he had a full load. Then he backed up and dumped it on the side of the path. It took more than an hour of this work before we arrived at the tree to be cut into usable log lengths.

I remember getting out of the warm pickup and catching my first breathe of the frigid air. I thought I was going to die. Dad picked up the chainsaw and worked on starting it, but without success. George climbed down from his tractor and fiddled with it, and it started. George could start anything.

It took Dad a few minutes of cutting before he produced the first usable logs. By that time, I was frozen stiff and wanted to go home, but the only way to go home was to fill the wagon with logs. Leslie and I both rushed to gather the logs and cast them over the tall wagon's side. It was the only way to keep warm was to throw logs and throw logs we did.

After two or three hours, we had all the logs that would fit on the wagon. It was heaped in the center so much that Dad had to drive behind the wagon when we headed home to ensure that no logs were lost.

When we arrived home, George backed the wagon to the basement window through which we tossed the logs into the basement. Since the window was on the south side of the house, we were protected from the winds. As long as we kept throwing logs into the basement, we were warm. After we finished emptying the wagon, Leslie parked it in its proper place and joined me in the basement to stack the logs. This was enjoyable because we were warm. We put the larger logs on the bottom and used logs of smaller diameters as we stacked towards the ceiling. When we finished and sealed the window, there was a sense of accomplishment and comfort. Having a basement filled with wood and corn cobbs was reassuring.

Grandpa and His Wood Working

When Grandpa was still a young man, he planted cedar trees in his pasture. Decades later, Grandpa cut them down and removed the branches from the trees. He transported them to his home site where he had a buzz saw. He powered it with the pulley of a tractor. He ran the trees through the buzz saw, which was a dangerous operation because there were no safeguards on the saw. He obtained planks that were from six to twelve inches in diameter.

Grandpa transported them to his haymow where he stacked them to dry. He placed six or eight planks side by side and then placed two spacer planks perpendicular to the planks he just laid out. This was to allow air to flow more readily among the planks.

They remained there for years. Every time a daughter or son was married, Grandpa climbed the stairs to the haymow and selected several of the best planks and took them to his wood shop on the first floor of the barn. There he had a table saw, a turning lay, and other basic tools. With these tools he built a cedar chest. When grandchildren were married, he continued his custom of building cedar chests, even though he was older and without much balance. I saw him sawing with the table saw as he braced himself against the barn's wall. Somehow, he managed to build most grandchildren a cedar chest.

Since I did not marry until later than my cousins, Grandpa could only give me the lumber. I had to push him up the stairs to the lumber in the haymow. I steadied him as he walked to the pile of lumber. He pointed at planks and told me to throw it out the haymow door. After he selected several planks, he confirmed that I had enough planks for the project. I guided him to the steps and helped him back down the steps. When my wife, Dona Katia, and I moved to our new house, I took the planks with me. I found a competent carpenter to build our cedar chest. He did so without the use of a single nail. Instead, he used wooden dowels. In the wood, we found two lead bullets that were placed there when my grandpa and uncles were hunting deer.

Also, with these tools, he built our house, Dad and Mom's walnut bed and a cedar lined closet for both. He built two fireplaces in our house. He built a clothes closet for Leslie and me and a dresser for Shannon. Grandpa was very self-sufficient.

1959 (12 years old, 7th grade)

More Land Added (4th Quarter)

Dad bought another quarter. It was located one mile farther from where two other quarters were situated. Since Dad bought it early in the year, he was able to have three wells dug with pumps and motors connected. They were powered by the 220 volts line.

In the spring, Leslie and I were disking and, even though we were only three hundred feet apart, there were times we could not see each other. This is more meaningful if you consider that we were sitting six feet up on a tractor seat. I could follow his progress by watching the JD 820's puff, puff, puff of black smoke coming from the diesel's muffler. That is a measure of how uneven the farm was when we bought it.

As soon as the farm was disked, it was flagged and surveyed. Dad moved several scrapers in to start the leveling process. It was slow because of the four-foot cuts and fills that were in many places. Where the cuts and fills were deep, Dad had the drivers remove the top six inches of topsoil and stockpile it, then they leveled the land. After it was declared level, the six inches of topsoil was replaced. This was because there were only approximately six inches of topsoil, after that, it was pure sand. Dad did not want to bury the topsoil and expose the pure sand.

One corner was filled with three acres of huge cottonwood trees. That area would remain uncultivated for a few more years. It would be expensive to convert now. Dad had already made a large investment.

Cutting Stalks

In the springtime, the first field operation was to cut stalks. Dad had welded together two two-row stalk cutters to obtain a four-row cutter. This was pulled the JD 60. My after-school job was to cut stalks. It was still early spring, but late enough that the soil was no longer frozen; a significant jacket was still required.

I rushed home after school and had my clothes changed before 3:45 p.m. Mom drove me to the quarter where I was currently cutting stalks. I started cutting stalks before 4:00 p.m. Since Leslie was covering for me, I did not have to do any chores.

It was pleasant hearing the JD engine putting along. The stalk cutter made a disconcertingly loud noise every time a blade penetrated the earth and cut the stalks. Then the turnstile would turn, and another burst of noise. My speed was only limited by what the implement could withstand. Since it was old, it could not withstand much, but I could travel at a comfortable speed.

Back and forth I went. I would allow my mind to wander, and I thought of many things. I watched proudly as I slowly marched across the field. Back and forth I went. That was one of the reasons I could never be a farmer. There was so much time wasted for the mind. While I was going back and forth, back and forth, my mind had nothing to do.

I decided I was not going home until I finished the field. I would be home late. Back and forth I went, and across the field I crept. The sun started to set. At first, the sun left an orange western sky, then it dimmed. Back and forth, back and forth, and the sky grew dark, and

I marched across the field. When it was dark, I turned on the tractor's lights. When the breeze blew from a given direction, it blew back onto me the engine's heat. That was welcome because it had grown very chilly in the transition from day to night.

I was hungry, but I could wait. I only had a couple of hours to go. Back and forth, back and forth I went. I loved watching the muffler. It spit out little red embers. I do not know why it would do that, but it did. Funny the things you notice at night that cannot be seen during the day.

Finally, I made my last round and headed home. I arrived home at 9:00 p.m. and ate supper, showered, and went to bed. I was too tired to do my homework.

This routine of going to the field as soon as Leslie and I arrived home from school was normal; although, we did not always work that late. Usually, we had time for our homework, but not much.

Cultivating with Gordon

In those days, we cultivated corn three or four times. Today, that is called "recreational tilling." We had hundreds of acres to cultivate. George used the four-row cultivator with the JD 730. He usually worked alone. Gordon and I worked as a team. We each had a JD B with a two-row cultivator. We sped along side by side and cover forty to sixty acres a day. The corn was taller with a sturdy stalk that made it difficult to cover with flying dirt. We were able to adjust the shields and open the throttle. We did this day after day after day.

Richard Timmons, Chemist

I do not know how Dick and Dad met, but Dad hired him to care for almost eight-hundred acres. His job included taking soil samples and testing them to discover which plant nutrients were in insufficient supply to raise a crop meeting Dad's desired yield, which was two or three times the land's average yield before he bought it. Included in Dick's recommendations were for a few ounces of zinc and a few more of molybdenum. Dad had a difficult time finding these compounds because no one else had used them. He went to the cooperative to ask for fertilizer with these compounds and all they could do was to scratch their heads.

Somehow, Dad found and applied these compounds to the corn crop. With the fertilizer, nutrients and micronutrients, Dad tripled the historical average yield on that farm. The neighbors were amazed.

Dick's job was not done. He visited the farm every four weeks to look for insects, insect eggs, and developing nutrient deficiencies. Sometimes, there was still time to correct a developing nutrient deficiency.

I was the official irrigator. It was my job to take him to each of the fields and go with him as he explored. Dick could not drive because he had lost his license when he was an alcoholic and drug user. Also, no one else wanted to go with him. His appearance showed the wear and tear of his early lifestyle. No one wanted to be near him. I liked Dick because he was super intelligent. He had a photographic memory. I would ask him a question about some insect or nutrient, and he told me that on his next visit he would bring me a book where on page xx and paragraph yy my question would be succinctly answered. And he did bring the book on his next trip and the question was answered.

While I normally walked around irrigating, if I saw an interesting insect, I captured it in a small box that I had found. I took it home at night and found Dad's book on insects that he bought from the University of Nebraska and learned about them. Some were helpful while others were detrimental. Sometimes, a week after a detrimental insect arrived, I found other insects that preyed on the bad insect. I started to see an entirely new ecosystem in the fields. There were so many things going on that most people never knew existed.

Dick kept telling me that he could get me into some good agricultural colleges around the Midwest. He told me about Iowa State University and Perdue University, and others. I thought he was blowing hot air because no one on the farm wanted to be near him but me. He also told me about when he was on a trip to Peru helping small farmers with their problems. He told me there was a large story about him on the front page of the nation's largest paper. I again thought he was blowing hot air. I never questioned his achievements, but I did doubt some of them. He also told me that he could get me a year either in Germany or Latin America studying in their agricultural colleges. That always excited me. I wanted to believe him, but I could not. That was a step too far. I could not imagine myself in a foreign country.

I could not simply discount what he said because he "reportedly" obtained his Doctorate in Chemistry in Austria during the 1930's. No one had ever seen his diploma. We only had his word that he had earned it. He told me that during World War II, he was on a submarine somewhere in the Pacific when there was a battle and what appeared to be an oil slick was left on the water. For reasons that were never made clear, the submarine was ordered to surface and take samples of the slick. After Dick took the samples, the submarine went straight to a U.S. port. Dick analyzed his samples. His conclusion was that they were no known chemicals from earth. Dick always had unusual experiences.

Years later, I visited his apartment. He showed me clippings from an old shoe box. On one of them was from Lima, Peru. On the front page was a photo of Dick doing something and I saw his name several times in the large article.

When I was studying at the College of Agriculture at the University of Nebraska, my advisor in soil science became very agitated one day when I mentioned Dick's name. My professor told me that Dick was a charlatan and probably only had a high school education. I mentioned that with his limited education he was tripling our corn yields. It took the University another fifteen years before it started to recommend zinc to farmers. Dick was special.

Taking a Lawn Mower Apart

I was always curious how a lawn mower's engine worked. As luck would have it, our old push mower stopped working. I decided I would dismantle the engine and learn why it was not working. I removed the spark plug and other things until I reached the piston. It was not too difficult to remove it, too. I found a host of other little things, which I removed and looked at. I had no idea what was wrong with it and lost interest in reassembling it. It remained dismembered. Dad was not happy.

The Milk and Cream Experiment

I spent weeks watching the cream separator separate the cream from the milk. On occasion when milking, the cream was thin and bountiful. Other occasions it was thick and scarce. I wondered if the cream separator was being consistent or if it was acting somehow randomly. I decided to document it.

I found a notebook and prepared a table to receive the results from weighing the milk and cream at each milking. I found a scale that could weigh buckets; even though, it did not have a good level of sensitivity. I weighed both the milk and cream at each milking and documented it by writing the numbers in the notebooks.

I maintained this practice for weeks. I did not know enough to find the percent of total milk produced was to the weight of the cream. I also did not know enough to make a line chart. That may have revealed some secret about cream and the milk cows' milk. I was frustrated because I wanted to learn more and did not know how to go about it.

Enter Hayes Randall

Dad had been looking to hire someone to help me with my work and to do random things around the farm. One day, Dad was in town at the cooperative gas station when he saw this idle man who was not young, but not old. It was Hayes Randall. Dad had an epiphany and asked Hayes what he was doing. Hayes replied that he was retired and doing nothing. Dad offered him a job and Hayes accepted. Hayes was lonely. His wife had died a while earlier.

Hayes and I did everything together. We removed barbed wire from fence posts because Dad no longer needed them. He wanted to plant on the land they occupied. First, we went down the line and removed all staples. Then we positioned the wire so that it could not hook on anything and with an attachment on the JD B's pulley, we pulled the half mile of wire and formed a neatly wrapped package of wire. We did these two or three times on the same fence until all the barbed wire was packaged. This was dangerous work because the pully applied much power to the wire and pulled it quickly. If the wire were to catch on something and snap, the end could fly into the air at great speed. It could do much damage to the human body.

Our next job was to take the JD 60 and put a manure loader on it because it had six-inch teeth on the end of it. The bottom part of the fence consisted of hog wire which was woven such that there were little rectangles between the various wires. Over the decades since the fence was installed, much soil had been blown by the winds. At least six inches of wire had been covered in soil and then in brome grass roots. No man was going to pull that fence out of the ground. It was stuck there.

That is when we positioned the loader and drove its teeth between the wires and lifted. Little by little the brome grass released its hold on the fence. This took time because we could only free about ten feet of fence with each positioning of the loader. We then hand-rolled the wire because it was now useless. People were taking down fences everywhere. No one was building them.

Sometimes Hayes went with Dad to survey a field. He also tilled the government set-aside acres. Whatever was asked of Hayes, he did it with a smile on his face and telling jokes to whomever would listen. I always enjoyed listening to his stories from when he was in high school.

Another task that Hayes and I did was to pick the field ends before it was harvested. That way Dad could turn the combine around without destroying any standing corn. Hayes and I picked about twenty feet back into the field. This was always an after-school job. The days were usually cool and refreshing. We had a Ford tractor with an old wagon with side boards on one side. This was so we could hit the wagon from twenty feet away. It gave us a larger target. We used the side boards as a bang-board.

My Legs Were Caught in Ford Tractor's Tires

Leslie, Gordon, and I were irrigating and using the Ford tractor for transportation. None of us was old enough to drive legally and sometimes the local sheriff's office patrolled rural areas seeking underage drivers who were irrigating. We had just finished making a set and were about to go to the next set. Leslie ran and jumped in the driver's seat. For Gordon and me, we were left with riding on the three-point hitch bar that did not have a stabilizer bar on it. That meant that the drawbar had at least six inches of horizontal movement in it. Leslie started driving, leaving us behind. Gordon beat me too the drawbar and secured himself with his hands to the driver's seat. A second later I caught up with the tractor, jumped onto the drawbar, and all I could secure with my hands was Gordon's waist. All my weight was being supported from Gordon's waist and the drawbar started to shift right, then left, then right again. When I shifted, it was even farther horizontally than the six inches from the drawbar's swing. In fact, I was becoming dangerously close to the tire, but we kept going and I refused to let go. Then the tire caught my buttocks and the tread pulled me farther up onto the tire. The tire's grips were slapping my bottom and each one pulled me closer to the top of the tire. Once I reached the top, there would be little that I could do to prevent from being pulled over and under the tire. I would have either been paralyzed or killed. Luckily, Leslie saw my predicament and locked the brakes. I fell to the ground behind the tire and remained there for a minute. I tried my legs, regained my motion, and stood up and shook my left leg. It was sore, but it worked fine. No one was laughing anymore. We all knew what almost happened. Gordon climbed on the left side of the drawbar, and I climbed on the right side of the drawbar, and we drove home at a reasonable speed.

That night I was quiet at supper, and no one noticed. After supper, I excused myself, took a hot shower and went to bed. The next day I was stiff and sore. We never talked any more about the incident.

Uncle Wayne's Lake and Sunday Fun

Uncle Wayne had a farm that was very sandy. A sand and gravel company wanted to receive the rights to remove sand and gravel. Uncle Wayne thought about it and granted their wish if they made it a certain shape and that it contained a small island. The sand pit ended up being a two-acre lake.

Uncle Wayne stocked the pond with Rainbow Trout and used it for fishing. He eventually invited Dad to join him. To make it interesting, Dad bought a small leisure boat with a large thirty-five horsepower engine. To prepare the facilities, we had a workday at the lake where a road was carved out of the brush, an outdoor toilet was dug, a picnic area was cleared from brush and a small dock was constructed. The lake was now open for business with one rule: everyone always wore a safety jacket while swimming or in the boat. This rule could never be broken.

Every Sunday after church, we loaded food and materials in the boat, and we were off to the lake. Uncle Wayne and his family were usually already there. Grandpa Tyler sometimes came to fish. He sat alone on the opposite side of the lake and quietly tried his luck. The rest of us swam and waterskied. We took turns driving the boat. Our motor was able to pull three people skiing if they took off from the dock. Some of the cousins: Kathy, Dan, and Brian; along with Joe tried forming a pyramid while skiing. They were good. It was fun.

Tippy did not enjoy remaining home alone. He figured out a way to jump into the boat and hide among all the equipment. When we left home, no one knew that he was there. After we had driven at least five or six miles, he left his hiding place and enjoyed the breeze on his face. He loved riding in the boat.

Grandpa Tyler and Fireworks

There was not a single child who liked fireworks on the 4th of July more than Grandpa Tyler. Grandpa had learned to eke out a living on the farm during the Great Depression. He learned to spend money only on essential supplies. Grandpa now considered fireworks essential supplies because he always had the biggest sack of them. This perhaps because he had gone so many years without being able to celebrate the 4th of July. He sat on the main side of the lake with the rest of the family while Joe and Leslie took all the fireworks to the far side of the lake and slowly set them off. It was beautiful watching them in the sky and seeing their reflections in the lake. Grandpa mostly enjoyed the oohs and aahs from the family members.

Grandpa Tyler's Orchard

Grandpa had an orchard between his house and Uncle Wayne's house. It was a wonderful and spacious area. It had blueberries, raspberries, strawberries, and blackberries. It also had cherries, apples, apricots, and peaches. The problem was that someone had to pick them. Dad always made Leslie and me go with Mom to pick. Like everything else, Mom was serious about picking and her hands were nimble and fast. I thought that this work was below me, not as important as driving a tractor. I did not like what I was doing but I had to do it anyway.

All the aunts also picked fruit from the orchard. Everyone always left a share at Grandma's house because picking fruit and berries was not work that she should be doing. They took their bounty home and we had fresh fruit and berries, plus they canned dozens of quarts for later consumption.

Dad Burns Weeds

Dad did whatever was necessary to make his scrapers more efficient. One problem was starting work on fields with large weeds. These weeds accumulated in the scraper bucket and were difficult to dislodge. While they were present, they diminished the scraper's capability to haul dirt. Dad developed a large weed burner. It burned on propane and cut a six-foot swath. He built a two-wheeled platform to carry the burner, which had a ten-foot reach from the platform.

When Dad started the burner, it was like firing up a jet engine. It was difficult to hear anything. Unfortunately, during those days we did not have noise reducing head gear. The wagon was pulled by the little Ford tractor.

Initially, Dad used me to drive the tractor, but he and I had philosophical differences. Dad would have both hands on the weed burner. He tried to tell me to stop, back up, go faster, slow down, start and many other orders by using his chin. I had no idea what he wanted. Sometimes Dad took one hand from the weed burner to help give me directions, but I had no idea what he wanted. Dad became angry. I became angry. We did not make good partners.

One lunchtime, I told him that I would no longer drive for him and was firm about it. I was surprised when Dad allowed me to resign. Meanwhile, he was working a large field with tall weeds, most of which was hemp, or marijuana. True, it was a low-grade marijuana, but it was still marijuana. Dad and a hired man spent all afternoon burning weeds. When he came home at night, rather than angry, Dad was happy. He laughed and joked and had the munchies. He could not wait for supper to eat.

Dad Built Grain Bins and Storage Units

All summer long, a series of large grain bins were being constructed. This included a large Quonset with the ability to store grain to more than eight feet deep. The boards used were eight feet long, but in the center the grain was even higher.

The building site was being expanded, but even so, it was becoming crowded.

Converting from Corn Picker to Combine

Dad wanted to minimize the time we spent harvesting our crops. Once they were ripe, every day the crops remained in the field was placing them at risk of a wind event or snowstorm. Speed was imperative. The old two-row corn picker was needing more and more repairs and could not be counted on to efficiently harvest the increasing number of corn acres. The Allis-Chalmers pull-combine also only harvested two rows of sorghum at a time. It was time to move up to a four-row harvester.

The self-propelled combine changed everything. The corn crib would remain empty. The ear corn elevator was parked deep in the trees. Now, Dad needed to find another way to dry the grain. The large and noisy fan in the corncrib, like the corncrib itself, was retired. Dad bought a 400-bushel propane batch drier. It was placed near the old corncrib. The JD 60 propelled it. It could usually dry about four hundred bushels every two hours. Given that that year's harvest progressed much faster than previously, the bottleneck was the drying procedure. The corn and milo came out of the field wetter than could be directly stored. It all had to be dried.

Now, a man and a truck had to be available at the farmstead. The man's job was to monitor the drying process so that he could empty the drier as soon as possible. He needed the truck to fill from the drier and then take to the steel bin where a large auger carried the corn into the bin. The drier always ran until late at night. Usually, my last task before bedtime was to turn off the drier. We could not just turn a switch and go away. I turned off the propane and left the fan running to cool the grain for fifteen minutes before I could turn off the drier and go to bed. I never minded this task because the smell was so pleasing. It did not matter if we were drying corn or milo, each had its own pleasing smell.

Another change involved the cattle Dad bought every fall. There would be fewer fallen ears because the self-propelled combine had a better system for grabbing the stalk and stripping the ear from it. There would be no more corn shelling. Mr. Rose's business just shrank. Also, the corn cobs were spread around the field rather than in the corral. They also could not be used in the house to start the wooden logs on fire. Dad quickly converted the house heating system to an electric system.

Helping Clark Williams Harvest Corn

One Friday night, Clark called Dad and asked if Leslie and I would be busy on Saturday. He wanted to hire us to help him harvest corn. Our harvest had just been completed. To my surprise, Dad consented. At 7:00 a.m. we were delivered to a spot on one of his farms that was a treed area, but it had an open space. Clark came and told me to stay put while he transported Leslie to another site. I am not sure what Leslie did for Clark.

When Clark returned, he helped me place a snow fence (long lathe sticks tied together by twisted wire) in a large circle with a diameter longer than thirty feet. He had me clean out the weeds inside the wire and then the corn started to arrive in wagons. My job was to unload the wagons and manage the corn falling inside the fenced enclosure.

I was running all day. Once I started the corn to fall from the wagon, I had to make sure that the elevator had the proper elevation, and that the enclosure was not overflowing. As soon as the corn level came within six inches of the top of the snow fence, I had to add another level of snow fence, a second story of corn. I had to hurry because the wagons that needed emptying were accumulating.

This routine continued until we reached the sixth story and the end of the day. By chance, the end of day arrived as we were filling the last story of the temporary corn crib. Clark wrote Leslie and me a check for seven dollars and fifty cents. We were exhausted, but happy with the money we had earned.

Grade School Basketball

I loved basketball and received permission from my parents to participate; however, there was a problem. Since the high school team used the gym after school, we had to practice before school started. The coach wanted to start practice at 7:00 a.m. I asked Mom and Dad to take me to practice. They refused. They thought it was the silliest thing of which they had heard. They were close to protesting to the school. I asked if I could ride my bicycle to school. They, at first, refused since it was dangerous to be riding a bicycle to school in the dark; it was early December. I persisted and, eventually, they gave in with one caveat: I had to have all the chores done before I left.

I set my alarm for 5:00 a.m. I quickly dressed for the cold, went to the cold barn, and milked the cows. It was hard because it was so dark and no one else was up yet, but I persisted. I finished milking the cows and haying the steers, dressed for school and prepared my practice bag. I climbed on my bicycle and balanced my practice bag on the handlebars and started toward school. Within fifteen minutes I parked my bicycle and joined my colleagues in the dressing room.

I maintained this program all during the basketball season. It continued to be a hot topic. I avoided talking about basketball at home.

Dick Vincent Joins the Scraper Team

In the spring, Dick started working for Dad by driving a scraper. He was a man in his mid-forties and mature. He was a serious driver and immediately became someone Dad trusted. He learned quickly how to make thin cuts and fills.

There were two types of scraper drivers. One type did the basic work by cutting the high ground and filling the holes. That does not imply that water would run as it should. These drivers did not have the "eye" for fine tuning the cuts and fills so that water would run. This was the second type of driver—the finisher. This person could see all the little cuts and fills that it took to make the water run without any puddles. This was the driver that allowed Dad to make the guarantee that water would flow without any of it standing in a pool. This was the group that Dick belonged. Dick had the magical touch. When he declared a lane done, it was done. It was almost impossible for Dad to survey and find that additional work was needed. Dick was invaluable.

Later that year, Dad bought a Letourneau D-Pull tractor on a twelve-yard scraper and gave it to Dick to drive. Dick was our finisher. It was his job to come across the lanes after everyone else had given up and finish the lane. Sometimes, the lane only needed a little work here and there, and sometimes it was a major challenge to finish it.

Emptying the Grain Quonset

Dad had to empty the grain from the Quonset to have a place to store this year's grain. A truck was parked outside the Quonset. One auger was brought to the front of the shed and placed in the milo. Milo was a horrible crop to move because it caused the skin to itch constantly.

Gordon and I were given the job of keeping the auger full. At first, this was not a problem because the auger ate its way to the floor and gravity did our work for us; but the grain was only about eight feet deep. Quickly we had to pull grain toward the auger and with only a slight delay we had to scoop. We were several feet into the building so there was no breeze, and it was a very hot summer day. Gordon and I stripped ourselves of our shirts and sweat like we were made of water. Since there were only two of us and the auger's capacity was considerable, we had to scoop nonstop. We only got a rest while they were switching out the trucks.

At the end of the day, I had to finish irrigating and then milk the cows, all the time while my body itched from the milo. I could not wait to be done so I could take a long shower.

I Was Nearly Electrocuted

Once, after a nice rain, Dad decided to empty a steel bin in preparation for the fall harvest. It was my job to make the preparations. The long auger had been previously positioned to remove grain, but I needed to move it sideways a little more. The electric motor was plugged into 220 volts. I picked up the end of the auger and pulled it away from the bin. The idea was that then I could back it up again and successfully placed the auger where it needed to be. The grass was very wet, it may have had a small amount of standing water. That was when I felt the shock. Somehow, the electric cord must have had a defect and when I pulled, I stretched it allowing a bare portion of the wire to contact the steel auger.

The result was that I started into a convulsion where I jumped up and down, slowly at first but after five or six up and downs, it tossed me high enough that my feet left the ground, and it threw me several feet. I was outside the water pool. I could not believe my luck because there were no other men working at home and Mom had no idea what I was doing.

Visitors from the City

The Sorensen's were from the Omaha area. Louie was an engineer on the Missouri River. Ginger was the wife. She was a fun-loving person who loved playing practical jokes on people, especially her husband. He was a very patient and quiet man. Ginger's parents had been excellent friends with Grandma and Grandpa Tyler. They used to visit Grandpa to hunt during hunting season.

Anyway, Ginger and Mom grew up together and were also excellent friends and by extension, Dad and Louie. They would often come to visit a day or two. They loved to see all the activity on the farm. Ginger and Louie had three children. The oldest, Christine, was beautiful, intelligent, and always very proper. She was two years older than me. Next was Kirk, he was about four years younger than I was. Finally, the youngest who was about six years younger than me.

For some reason that morning, I was responsible for grinding all the ingredients for the steers' feed and feeding them. I had the JD 60 and grinder. I backed it to an old shed where oats were held. I positioned the auger and its catch area so that it was the perfect distance and placement from where I would be throwing it from inside the building. I started the auger. The JD 60 was at full throttle. I had to step into a room, fill my scoop, step back and throw the oats out the shed door and into the auger. I had to keep pace with the auger. It was never good to allow an auger to run dry. I had developed a rhythm stepping into the next room, filling my scoop, stepping back, and throwing the oats into the auger. I was matching the auger perfectly. I kept the catch pan full so that the auger doing its pulling the grain from under it looked like a blender working on a full load of ingredients.

Suddenly, when I stepped back and threw a load of oats at the auger, I see little Kirk there, staring at the auger and preparing to stick his hand in to see what is making it move. I stopped and leapt from four feet up where I was working and knocked him to the ground. He started crying and walked back to the house. I had a dry auger, so I had to return immediately to my work.

Several minutes later, when I stepped back to throw oats at the grinder, I saw Mom walking directly toward me in triple time and with purpose. Behind her, and losing ground with each step, was Ginger. Mom arrived and started yelling at me. I could not hear her, so I stepped out of the grain shed and stopped the tractor, slowing its throttle.

Kirk told her how I had knocked him to the ground and left him. Eventually, when Ginger caught up with Mom and I had quieted Mom, I explained how, if I had waited one second more, Kirk would not have a right arm and might, in fact, be dead. After a brief period of silence, Ginger thanked me while Mom turned and double-timed it back to the house. Mom never strolled or walked. He normal speed was double-time. She always had work waiting for her somewhere.

1961 (14 years old, Freshman)

Loading the Corn Planter

Every spring brought corn planting. Last year's corn stalks had been disked twice and harrowed leaving a smooth and soft planting bed. George's job was to use the JD 730 and a four-row planter to plant the corn. Once planting, speed was imperative to avoid possible bad weather. The greatest limiting factor to the number of acres planted in a day was the time it took every couple of rounds to resupply the planter with seed and fertilizer.

That is where I came in. We had a pickup filled with sacks of seed and a wagon filled with sacks of fertilizer. On George's last row before resupplying, it was my job to back the pickup to align with where George would park. I also positioned the fertilizer wagon. I took the necessary sacks of seed, opened them, and positioned them close to where the planted would park. I did the same for fertilizer. When George parked the planted, it only took a couple of minutes to resupply the planter. I pulled the wagon out of George's way and George was off. With this operation, George significantly increased the number of acres planted in a day.

Shop Teacher Worked for Dad

During the summer of 1961, Dad hired another man to drive a scraper. This happened to be the shop teacher that would be teaching me wood working in the fall. There he was, working beside me. Both of us covered in dust going back and forth in the field cutting and filling. Suddenly, it was the last Saturday before school started. We had just returned from a dusty day on the tractors. Before he got into his car, he said, "I believe I will be seeing you on Monday. All I could say was, "Yes, sir!" I was apprehensive about entering high school. Our high school was huge. It had at least one hundred students and we would be interacting with all of them. At least I already knew one of my teachers.

I Entered High School

That fall, I entered high school. That meant that I moved up one floor since high school was on the top floor. I learned what a "home room" was and to move from classroom to classroom as our classes changed. It was my first experience with male teachers. It was a lot of new things, but I liked it.

Our algebra teacher, Mrs. Shonsey, was fantastic. I always had heard of the magic of algebra, and I wanted to discover it. She was so organized and each day she presented new material that I craved to learn. It was the same way for each class, and each teacher gave much homework. At night, I felt overwhelmed with all that I had to do, but I was happy to be learning so much.

Our shop teacher was excellent. He was serious and direct. There would be no funny business in his class. Each day he explained a new concept, then we worked on our projects.

Each teacher gave daily homework assignments that required time to complete. My one study hall gave me a chance to complete one class's homework. The others I took home with me. I always had my hands full of books. After working on the farm for a couple of hours, doing my chores, and eating supper, and I started to study. This was usually after 7:00 p.m. I was constantly worrying about completing all my assignments.

Leslie Receives Driver's License

In February, Leslie received his driver's license. Dad allowed him to buy a 1959 Chevrolet Biscayne. It was a simple car, but we thought of it with fondness because it allowed us to drive to school rather than ride the school bus. It gave us more freedom.

Land Leveling

John Deere changed their style of tractor radically from the JD 830 to the JD 4010. Dad bought one to pull a new Hancock twelve-yard scraper. It had seventy-two horsepower and pulled the scraper easily. It was a beautiful and compact tractor. It was a technological marvel compared to the old JD 830. Everyone fought for the honor to drive it.

When Leslie and I were busy driving scrapers or irrigating or otherwise occupied, Dad took the girls to carry surveying rods on surveying jobs. Shannon was twelve, Shelli was ten, and Sheri was eight. Shannon and Shelli were expected to carry a ten-foot rod. Sheri was allowed to carry the eight-foot rod.

Dad set up his instrument in the middle of the field. He dropped the girls off with their rods. Shannon, being the oldest, was expected to count steps to estimate the one-hundred feet intervals. The other girls would line up on her position before placing their flags and holding the rod still while Dad read the height threw his instrument. When Dad finished reading Shannon's rod and wrote it down, he waved, and she started counting as she walked to the next flag's position. Dad then focused on Shelli and again waved when he was done. The same for Sheri.

This left many chances for problems to occur. If each girl was not paying close attention, one might fail to walk after Dad waved, or two girls may think Dad was waving to them and walk before Dad had finished reading their rod. This caused Dad to invent hand signals to indicate what the girls, and which girl, was supposed to do. When the girls did not understand, Dad became more and more frustrated until he jumped into the pickup and pushed the foot feed to the floor, throwing dust thirty feet behind the pickup. The pickup left a large trail of dust behind it. It was frequently no fun to work for him, especially when it involved trying to interpret his made-up hand signals.

The Spanish Book

Once, I was on a job west of Central City with Dick Vincent. It was a big job and I had settled in to working on a hundred-foot lane that was going to take much more than a day to complete and there were many more lanes like that one. The temperature was hot, but comfortable. Each time we loaded the scraper, we kicked up a cloud of dust that settled on ourselves and left our faces and hair full of dirt.

Before we ate, we tried to clean the area around our mouths from as much dust as we could. Then, we ate our lunch under the shade of trees that were part of the building site, which was very old and long since abandoned. It had a house with the door open and many of the windows broken out. After finishing my lunch, I walked into the house and walked around. There was an old calendar on the wall that may have indicated the year the house was abandoned.

There on the floor of one of the rooms was an old Spanish book. I picked it up. I had always wanted to learn to speak Spanish, but our school system did not offer it at any level. I opened the book. It seemed easy to read and understand. I decided to keep it and packed it in my now empty lunch bucket. A few years later, I took it with me when I lived in El Salvador. It helped me to become fluent in Spanish.

Fixing the Brake on a JD B

One of the brakes stuck on the JD B and it drove me nuts. Every time I pushed it, it worked, but it would not return to its original position. I had to reach down and pull it back. I could manage doing it once or twice, but not a hundred times. I was determined to fix it. I parked it in an area in the shop, opened the brake and removed it. I found an area of the brake that was rough and decided to smooth it. I located some emery paper and rubbed it for several minutes until it was smoother. I put everything back together and evaluated it. It worked. I was impressed with myself.

1963 (16 years old, Sophomore)

A Summer's Date

I am a shy person. To finally have a Saturday night date was important. I was excited all week and looking forward to Saturday. When Saturday finally came, I arose at 5:00 a.m., determined to finish my work early so I could have a normal date. I milked the cows and started irrigating as soon as the sun showed its face. I had completed checking half of my first sets when I went in for breakfast. I ate quickly and was back to checking irrigation sets.

By lunch time, I had completed half of my second irrigation sets. I ate a quick dinner and returned to irrigating. I completed my evening sets and milked the cows. I was on pace for an early shower and departure. That was when I was informed that the other irrigator was far behind in his sets and needed help. It took two hours to help complete his tasks.

After eating supper and cleaning up, it was 8:30 p.m. I did not arrive to pick up my date until 9:00 p.m. We never left her place. I was exhausted and headed home at 10:00 p.m. I went straight to bed, disappointed. On a farm, your work is never done until the last person's work is done.

Dad Sells the Milk Cows

Weeks before Leslie graduated from high school, Dad informed us that he was selling the milk cows. I was elated until I had a moment to think about it. I had known these cows for years. I knew their personalities and moods, and they knew mine. It was especially difficult to watch as they were loaded into the truck and knowing their destiny. I was very sad. Suddenly, I did not want them to leave. I would milk them and not complain, but it was too late. They were gone.

Leslie Graduates from High School

Leslie graduated from high school that spring. He spent the summer working on the farm. In the fall, he attended an electronics school in Denver, Colorado. In May, I received my driver's license. That allowed me to go to town on Saturday night and would allow me to drive me and my sisters to school in the fall.

1964 (16 years old, Junior in High School)

We Buy More Land (5th and 6th Quarters)

During early 1964, Dad found 320 acres of undeveloped land (the Dunn place) and arranged for Leslie and me to buy it. It was located five miles north of our homestead, on the ridge marking the end of the Platte Valley. Even so, the soil was extremely sandy, very uneven with a water table at least sixty feet deep.

Dad sunk several irrigation wells and surveyed both quarters. It was going to be a gigantic project to level for gravity irrigation. It was very hilly, and the soil was sandy. He was busy with projects. If it rained on a project making it impossible to scrape, to keep the drivers employed, he transferred them our new farm. Since our soil was sandy, they could work immediately. Little by little our farm was leveled because it was always raining on one project or another.

The deepest cut was nine feet, and the deepest fill was five feet. With topsoil no deeper than six to eight inches deep, all topsoil would be either cut off or filled over with sand, thus we would destroy all the topsoil. Instead, Dad had all topsoil removed and stacked in a pile. Then the drivers leveled the sand. Once the sand was level with the proper gradient, they went to the topsoil pile and spread it about six inches deep across the previously leveled land.

Once the land leveling was complete, Dad brought in Dick Timmons to analyze the soil and make recommendations. As usual, his recommendations included zinc and molybdenum. Dad followed his recommendations, and we tripled the farm's yield the first year.

High School Bomb Making

In the spring of 1964, I was a junior in high school. The school only offered four classes for me. The rest of the time was study hall. I quickly did my school assignments and then I had nothing to do, so I started to think. I thought and thought. I decided I was going to make a small bomb at home and put it in the desk belonging to the English teacher. I would set the timer to go off during freshman English class. And I knew exactly how I was going to make it.

At home, I found an old broom and cut it into one-foot lengths. I wrapped crate paper diagonally around each piece and glued it to each broom stick piece. I found an old alarm clock and a huge battery that belonged to the old telephones that we rang using a handle on the side of the phone. I pounded a nail into one end of each wood piece and wrapped wires around each nail. I then strung wires from the old battery and the alarm clock and connected them. I was done. It looked quite real.

When no one was looking, I placed the box containing the bomb in the second drawer of the English teacher's desk and closed it. It was set for a few minutes into class.

A few minutes after the alarm rang, I was in study hall doing nothing because I had nothing to do. The huge principal came to the door and looked straight at me and smiled as he extended his wide hand and wiggled his finger for me to go to him. Suddenly, I was afraid. I followed him up the stairs to his office. He closed the door and asked me to sit down. On another chair I saw my bomb. He was still smiling, but it was a smile that transmitted fear and I was suddenly very serious and afraid. He asked, "Is that yours?" I answered that it was. He said, "do not do it again. Pick it up after school and I do not want to see it again." With that, he waved his hand away from him signaling me that the meeting was over, and I should vacate the premise.

I have often wondered how he knew that I was the one who made the bomb. There was no investigation. He walked right to me. Somehow, he knew. I did not understand.

1965 (17 years old, Senior)

Unloading Trucks during School Time

Clark Williams was a local large farmer and businessman. In addition to farming, he sold fertilizer and seed corn. Seed corn came in fifty-six-pound sacks (one bushel) and fertilizer came in one-hundred-pound sacks. In the spring, Clark would receive semi after semi of loads of corn seed and the several types of fertilizer. Sometimes, he had no spare men to unload the trucks. He would call the high school and request four strong students. The superintendent would locate four seniors with two consecutive study halls and send them out to Clark's farm. I was usually one of them since I had a car and could drive. When we finished, Clark wrote a check to each of us. We were happy and felt special.

Irrigation

We had trouble holding the irrigation ditches on the Dunn place. The soil was so sandy that we could not keep the water inside the ditches. Leslie and I bought a mile of irrigated pipe. We laid it in the place of the former ditches. The sand could no longer melt away, and we could take the water down a slight slope and up the other side without involving the levelers. We did not have to worry about ditch breaks or digging out rows or which size tube to use because we could simply adjust the length of the open gate. It was marvelous. It saved so much time.

Post High School Graduation

I had applied to the University of Oklahoma. Why? Because it was 450 miles south of Clarks, Nebraska and would be several degrees warmer than in Nebraska on any given day. After a few weeks there, I decided that I should take some agricultural classes. I went to the registrar to obtain a course catalog for their College of Agriculture.

The people laughed at me and told me I had the wrong university. The only agricultural classes offered in the state were in Oklahoma State University. Apparently, Oklahoma University had a superiority complex with Oklahoma State University. I wish we had had better orientation in high school. If we would have had orientation in high school, I wonder if I would have listened. I was a bit stubborn and tended to do what I wanted regardless of what other people told me.

George Takes Care of My Sisters

After I graduated from high school, Shannon started driving the car to school. Every day, George pulled the car around and parked next to the door to the house. He ensured that the car always had gasoline. During the winter, George left the car running so that it would be warm for the girls. He scraped the windows to guarantee that they were clear. He also kept tract of the mileage and periodically changed oil in the car. During the five years that one of my sisters was driving a car to school, George never missed a day of having the car ready and in front of the house door. George was a saint.

www.ingramcontent.com/pod-product-compliance
Lightning Source LLC
LaVergne TN
LVHW091933070526
838200LV00068B/951